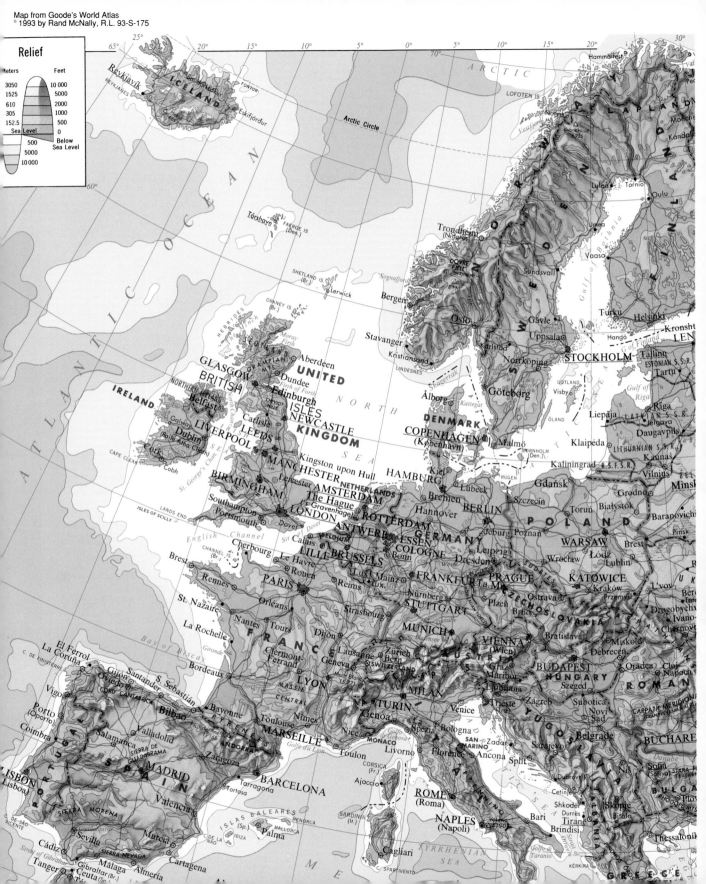

Map from Goode's World Atlas
© 1993 by Rand McNally, R.L. 93-S-175

Enchantment of the World

DENMARK

By Martin Hintz

Consultant for Denmark: Albert Larson, Ph.D., Assistant Professor,
Department of Geography, University of Illinois at Chicago, Illinois

Consultant for Reading: Robert L. Hillerich, Ph.D., Professor Emeritus,
Bowling Green State University, Bowling Green, Ohio;
Consultant, Pinellas County Schools, Florida

 CHILDRENS PRESS®
CHICAGO

Farmhouse reflected in a pond

Project Editor: Mary Reidy
Design: Margrit Fiddle

Library of Congress Cataloging-in-Publication Data

Hintz, Martin.
    Denmark / by Martin Hintz.
    p.   cm. – (Enchantment of the world)
    Includes index.
    Summary: Discusses the geography, history, government, people, and culture of this Scandinavian country.
    ISBN 0-516-02620-8
    1. Denmark–Juvenile literature. [1. Denmark.]
I. Title. II. Series.
DL109.H56   1994   93-35487
948.9–dc20   CIP
                                                         AC

Picture Acknowledgments
AP/Wide World Photos: 38, 39, 41, 42, 92, 93 (left)
Culver Pictures: 29, 33, 34, 35, 37, 80, 81, 83, 84 (right)
GeoImagery: © Erwin C. Bud Nielsen, 4, 11
H. Armstrong Roberts: © R. Kord, 22; © P. Degginger, 46 (top); © Blumebild, 50 (right); © A. Tovy, 59 (right)

Chip and Rosa Maria de la Cueva Peterson: 6 (top left), 9 (right), 10, 16, 17, 43, 49 (top), 52 (right), 57 (2 photos), 67, 70 (right), 88, 90 (right), 97 (right), 104, 109 (left)
Photri: 59 (left), 60, 61 (left), 93 (right), 99: © Erik Betting, 6 (bottom), 9 (left), 21, 55 (left); © Foto Betting, 8; © Christian Titlow, 12; © Claus Petersen, 46 (bottom), 69 (bottom left), 82; © J. Novak, 51 (right), 71; © Bo Jarner, 54 (left), 70 (left), 101 (left); © Jesper Hyllemose, 56 (left); © Gunvor Jørgsholm, 61 (right); © Ann Bang, 66; © Sisse Jarner, 78, 97 (left); © Mikael Hjuler, 90 (left), 94, 102 (left); © Lisbeth Hedland, 102 (right)
© **Ann Purcell:** 58 (left)
© **Carl Purcell:** 58 (right), 76 (bottom), 109 (right)
Root Resources: © Russel A. Kriete, 51 (left), 108
© **Bob and Ira Spring:** 75, 111
Stock Montage: 26 (2 photos), 84 (left)
Tony Stone Images: © Rohan, Cover; © Robert Everts, 53; © Karen Phillips, 56 (right)
SuperStock International, Inc.: © Schuster, 6 (top right); © Steve Violer, 24, 52 (left); © A. Tessore, 49 (bottom); © Bill Curtis, 50 (left); © Hubertus Kanus, 55 (right); © Kurt Scholz, 62; © Eric Carle, 69 (top left)
Travel Stock: © Donna Carroll, 5, 18, 54 (right), 68, 76 (top), 91 (left); © Buddy Mays, 14, 15 (2 photos), 63 (2 photos), 69 (right), 73, 91 (right), 103
Valan: © Kennon Cooke, 101 (right); © Jean-Marie Jro, 105
Len W. Meents: Maps on 7, 11, 47, 55, 60, 62, 63
Courtesy Flag Research Center, Winchester, Massachusetts 01890: Flag on back cover
Cover: Copenhagen, Nyhavn tour boat

A woman prepares smorrebrod, *the open-faced sandwiches that are popular in Denmark.*

TABLE OF CONTENTS

Top left: An aerial view of the northern tip of Jutland   Top right: Ronne is the capital, port, and largest town on the island of Bornholm.   Above: Mykines is a tiny atoll of the Faeroe Islands with a population of about thirty people.

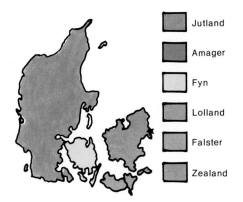

Jutland

Amager

Fyn

Lolland

Falster

Zealand

Chapter 1

ENFOLDED BY THE SEA

The peninsular western part of Denmark thrusts into the stormy waters of the North Sea like a large fist. Totaling 16,633 square miles (43,080 square kilometers), it clings to the European mainland and borders Germany to the south. It has a coastline of 1,057 miles (1,701 kilometers). The main landmass, which covers about 70 percent of Denmark, is called Jutland.

Denmark also comprises numerous offshore islands. Among the major islands are Zealand, Fyn, Lolland, Falster, and Amager, as well as another 450 smaller pinpoints of land. Bornholm, a large island, lies 80 miles (129 kilometers) east. It is closer to Sweden than is other Danish territory. The Faeroe Islands and Greenland, which lie far to the northwest, are also part of Denmark.

The country is swept by ocean winds. It has a relatively mild climate because it is washed by the warm North Atlantic Current. However, when ice blocks the Baltic Sea to the east near the Danish island of Bornholm, the warm waters are cut off. Severe winters with bone-chilling cold result.

Danish farmers use efficient techniques to work their rich farmlands.

The Ice Age, which lasted tens of thousands of years, shaped today's Denmark. Most of the surface of present-day Denmark is the result of deposits by huge glaciers that once scraped the earth's northern landscape and left deposits of rock and gravel when they melted. Since that time, wind and rain have modified Denmark's face even more.

The vast sea continually scrubs the shoreline, shifting the sand dunes and wearing away the rocky spits offshore. In fact, there was once a land bridge between Jutland and the Scandinavian peninsula to the north. This rib of rock disappeared centuries ago under the wave action and the rising sea.

Denmark today is a land of rolling, well-worn hills and lowlands. The highest point is Yding Skovhoj in Jutland at 568 feet (173 meters). The lowest is below sea level along the west coast. Here extensive dikes hold back the seawater, and rich farmland that once was below the surface of the water has been reclaimed.

*The longest river in Jutland is the Guden (left)
and there are many small picturesque lakes (right).*

The longest river, the Guden in Jutland, stretches only 98 miles
(158 kilometers). There are many small lakes, especially in central
Jutland. A canal connects the town of Odense on Fyn with
Odense Fjord, making the town a seaport. A *fjord* is an inlet of
the sea between steep hills.

Denmark's climate is temperate, with an average of 32 degrees
Fahrenheit (0 degrees Celsius) in January and 62 degrees
Fahrenheit (16.6 degrees Celsius) in July. Strong winds continually
brush across the country because there are no mountains for
protection. A Danish winter is usually cool, cloudy, and humid
instead of snowy and cold, unlike that of some of its
Scandinavian neighbors. Summer is a brighter time with
alternating sunshine and clouds. Total rainfall averages about 24
inches (61 centimeters) per year.

About 9 percent of Denmark is forested, but there are no large
tracts of forests. Beech, fir, elm, maple, oak, and ash trees are
scattered across the hills. Most of the country, about 73 percent, is

A typical Danish farmstead

cultivated. Danish farmers are proud of their croplands, which produce turnips, sugar beets, and thick stands of hay, oats, and barley. Cattle, pigs, sheep, and chickens are raised and used in the production of high-quality food products.

All this cultivation doesn't leave much room for wild animals, but there are foxes, squirrels, rabbits, ducks, partridges, and pheasants, as well as a few deer. To see anything more exotic, Danish children enjoy going to the zoo.

THE POPULATION AND LANGUAGE OF DENMARK

The population in Denmark totals more than five million people. Among the largest cities are Copenhagen, Odense, Århus, and Ålborg. The metropolitan area of Copenhagen, the capital, accounts for more than 1,300,000 persons. Zealand, the island on which most of the city is located, holds almost 40 percent of the

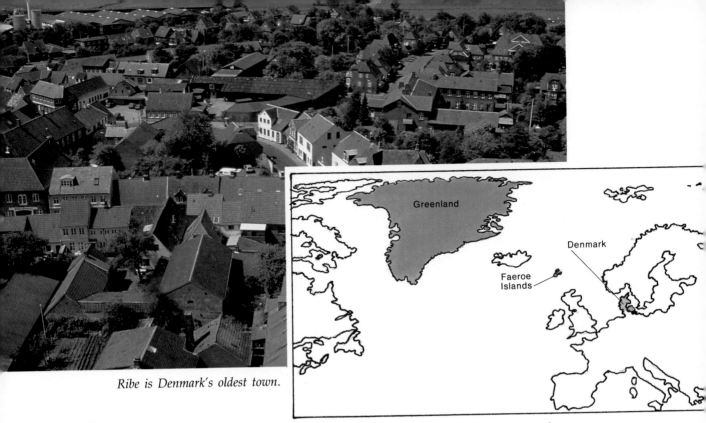

Ribe is Denmark's oldest town.

population. Most Danes, however, live in smaller towns with populations of 50,000 or less.

The official language throughout the land is Danish, although English is spoken everywhere.

THE FAEROE ISLANDS

The volcanic Faeroe Islands are located northwest of Scotland. There are eighteen main islands in the craggy chain and four smaller uninhabited specks of rock, spread out over 540 square miles (1,399 square kilometers). The land consists of mountains and rock-strewn valleys. Fjords cut into the coastlines of the islands.

The islands have names such as Koltur, Hestur, Mykines, Streymoy, and Nolsoy. Because they are washed by the North Atlantic Current, there is a climate of cool summers and mild

Ruins of the thirteenth-century Magnus Cathedral in the Faeroe Islands

winters. There are few great changes in temperature in the winter and summer. Heavy fog often rolls over the islands. But when the thick mist clears, brilliant blue skies explode over the rough gray-green seas. During the winter, thick snow packs the mountain ridges and extends to the rocky shore. Spring brings alive carpets of dazzling crimson, white, and yellow wildflowers.

The Faeroes were populated as early as A.D. 800 by Irish monks, who appreciated their solitude and rugged beauty. Norsemen drove the monks from their monasteries and then settled the outlying islands. The Faeroes remained independent until 1036, when they came under the rule of Norwegian kings. In 1380 a Norwegian-Danish monarchy assumed control. But even royalty could not help when the Black Death, a horrible plague that swept Europe during the Middle Ages, almost wiped out the entire population. After the epidemic, the Faeroes were repopulated by adventurous Norwegian settlers whose descendants are still on the islands. When the union between Norway and Denmark was dissolved in 1814, the Faeroes kept their link with Denmark.

In the 1800s a nationalist movement tried to break away from the parent country. One of the popular ideals of the rebels was to revive the original Faeroese language. While their political movement collapsed, they were successful in reestablishing the popularity of Faeroese. However, all adults also speak Danish, which is a compulsory subject taught in the schools.

GREENLAND

Greenland (Kalaallit Nunaat) is the world's largest island, unless Australia is considered an island as well as a continent. Greenland is almost totally within the Arctic Circle. Geographically part of North America, it sprawls across 840,000 square miles (2,175,600 square kilometers). Greenland is 1,660 miles long (2,671 kilometers) from north to south. At its widest point, generally in the midsection of the island, it is about 750 miles (1,207 kilometers) from east to west.

Greenland is bounded by the Arctic Ocean on the north, the Greenland Sea on the east, the Denmark Strait on the southeast, the Atlantic Ocean on the south, and Davis Strait and Baffin Bay on the west.

Vast glaciers still edge down from the mountain ranges that crisscross the island parallel to the east and west coasts. Mount Gunnborns, located in southeast Greenland (12,139 feet; 3,700 meters), is the highest elevation.

About 85 percent of Greenland is covered by an immense sheet of ice. The glaciers that cover the interior are at least 14,000 feet

Summertime in Greenland

(4,267 meters) thick in some places. By drilling deep into the cores of the glaciers and removing samples, scientists have been able to study the world's climate over the past 100,000 years. Tests show there are actually three islands beneath the extensive glacier. Glacier ice moves outward from its origin, ending up in the sea, where huge chunks fall into the ocean to form icebergs. They often drift into sea lanes, causing a hazard for shipping.

Due to Greenland's size, its climate ranges from constant cold in the north to milder conditions along the south coast, washed by the North Atlantic Current. Frigid winds roar out of the interior to mingle with the warmer air around the coasts. This mixture causes thick fog, adding to the iceberg danger when travelers approach Greenland by sea. While there may be deep snow on the northern portion of Greenland, heavy rains often sweep the southern part of the island.

There are no forests on Greenland. Only stunted trees can be

Scenes from Greenland: salmon drying on racks (left) and a fisherman with his son (right)

found along the southern coast. Natural vegetation, in a region called the *tundra*, consists mostly of moss, lichens, and grass.

Greenland was given its name by Eric the Red, a Norseman from Iceland, who established the first colony there around A.D. 982. (Until Iceland gained independence in 1944, it belonged to Denmark.) This was an early example of creative advertising. Eric made the name attractive to lure subsequent settlers. The Eskimos, or Inuit, who had lived on Greenland for at least four thousand years, could have told the Norse stories about the difficulties of living there. But Eric's tales worked well at home. By the twelfth century, about four thousand robust pioneers from Iceland lived on Greenland along with their Inuit neighbors.

Polar bears, musk oxen, wolves, lemmings, arctic foxes, and reindeer live on Greenland, with numerous varieties of sea birds. Fishing for cod, halibut, and salmon and the hunting of seals are major industries. Sheep are raised along the southern tip.

North of Copenhagen is the Frilandsmuseet, *an open-air museum in which farms represent different regions and periods in Danish history.*

BELIEF IN NATURE AND CONSERVATION

For centuries, the Danish landscape has been molded by men and women who augmented nature's work. Only the seacoast of Denmark can be considered much the same as it was when people first settled here, except for the reclaimed lands along the west coast. Immediately upon their arrival, the people began to shape and change the earth. Fields were divided by hedges of shrubs. Pastureland was carved out of forests. Today's environmentalists are concerned that the Danish landscape is taken too much for granted.

Streams have been straightened, wetlands and bogs drained, and ponds filled. This is often done in the name of helping the economy. However, younger Danes remember their history lessons. They look back at the sixteenth century when Denmark's great forests were cut down and used as masts and planks for

The Nature Conservation Association of Denmark sponsors much environmental legislation to preserve the country's lands.

ships. Danes fear that their country is now undergoing another ecological attack.

Yet even in the past, not everyone turned a deaf ear to the problem. There was help. In 1805, the first forest preserves were established to protect what was left of the timberland. Zoologists and botanists fought hard in the middle of the nineteenth century to preserve the remaining heath and bogs that were going to be turned into farms. The Heath Society, which was formed then, reclaimed forestland in west Jutland. In 1911, the Association for Nature Conservation in Zealand and the Southern Islands was founded. Its activities expanded nationwide and the name was eventually changed to the Nature Conservation Association of Denmark. Its hardworking members have sponsored protective environmental legislation.

Special Danish conservation courts were set up in 1917 to determine the best use of the land. These courts have often had to

Much of the coastline has been protected from overdevelopment.

limit the rights of individual landowners who wanted to develop their property. Building restrictions are in effect, preventing construction along large streams, around lakes, and near historic sites. These regulations have protected most of the country's coastline.

However, these early laws have often proved inadequate to control modern growth and the land-hungry demands of a growing population. So several new laws were passed in the 1960s and 1970s to provide increased protection for many areas. The establishment of a "preservation order" is sometimes necessary to safeguard a particular area.

Experts are called in to determine the value of the land from an environmental and economic standpoint. After studying the findings of the researchers, the minister of the environment can impose a temporary ban on any construction. At that time, a central conservancy board holds a public hearing on the matter. Danes are skilled debaters, so everyone offers an opinion. After all the facts are taken into consideration, the board rules on what should be done. Compensation is paid to the landowner if it is ruled necessary to let the land alone.

Unlike some other countries, these protected areas often include a mixture of villages, sites for vacation cottages, and farmland, as well as undeveloped property. About 3.5 percent of Denmark's total land has subsequently been protected. Nine scientific reserves such as the Cliffs of Mon and the Jutland Heath, as well as seventy-five wildlife preserves, have been established since the early 1980s.

Industrial and urban pollution has been a problem in Denmark just as it has been in most other countries. However, under tough environmental protection laws now in effect, polluters have to clean up their messes.

Koge Bay, near Copenhagen, was once a vast pool of dirty, trash-filled water. Under the regulations, sewage is purified before being discharged into the bay. Factories are prevented from unloading chemicals and waste into the water. The bay is now clean and has become a major recreation area.

Environmental protection is now being taken more seriously in Denmark. Denmark remains a leader among European nations, seeking a balance between the important needs of its citizens today and those of tomorrow.

Chapter 2

A PEOPLE FASHIONED BETWEEN ROCK AND WATER

Tens of thousands of years ago, glaciers covered much of present-day Denmark. The surface was packed with sheets of ice hundreds of feet thick. Over the centuries, this ice regularly advanced and then melted back. This allowed animals and people to live along the fringes of the ice and follow its movement. They simply migrated out of the way when the weather turned cold and the glaciers turned their frosty faces south again.

Eventually, the great ice packs melted completely from the Danish peninsula. This allowed hardy nomad hunters to prowl throughout the entire peninsula. Artifacts of these early humans, dating back to the third and fourth ice ages, have been found in remote reaches of south Jutland. The most recent finds are from about five thousand years ago. Remains of villages also have been found at the edges of ancient lakes. These were probably summer homes, close to excellent fishing holes.

As early as 3000 B.C., the hunters finally settled down permanently. They grew cereal grains, using the *ard*, a clumsy

Troldkirken, *"Troll Church,"* one of Denmark's oldest primitive shrines

wooden plow, to till the hard soil. Skilled archaeologists, reading today's landscape like a book, have found traces of their fields. These farmers lived in longhouses and small circular homes made of logs and stone. They were skilled at shaping flint into beautiful knives and spears.

Primitive shrines still dot the Danish countryside, dating from these years. One of the oldest is at *Troldkirken* (Troll Church) on a hilltop near Limfjord. A low heap of rocks is encircled by higher stones. Inside the circle, religious ceremonies were held. A huge stone rests in the center of the circle, where sacrifices probably were made.

The Lur Blower Column,
with two Vikings blowing
ancient trumpets,
stands at Town Hall
Square in Copenhagen.

BRONZE AGE DANES

During the Bronze Age (1500-500 B.C.), the harsh honking of the *lur*, an ancient trumpet, echoed across the windswept land. Worshipers gathered for religious ceremonies, called together by the haunting sounds of the horns. Several of these musical instruments have been found in burial pits and can still be played.

Numerous graves from this time have been reopened, providing a fascinating peek into the Danish past. The oldest surviving clothing in Europe has been recovered from oak coffins in Denmark, preserved by tannin in the wood. Girls of the day apparently wore short-sleeved blouses and short corded skirts, with large belt plates. Women usually wore ankle-length dresses.

In a burial mound at Borum Eshoj, a man's kilt, cloak, and stitched cap were found. Folding stools, drinking horns, and boxes were often placed with the dead person for the long, cold trip into the afterworld.

Ancient Danes met and traded with travelers from faraway lands. From these encounters, about 500 B.C., they learned the value of iron, which was harder than their bronze tools. New architectural styles and new crop-raising techniques were adopted. The Danes even copied the use of trousers from their Celtic neighbors to the south. From other tribes, they learned to fashion ornate silver goblets and bowls.

We know how these men and women looked from the face of the Tollund Man, found in a grave dating back two thousand years. Despite the quiet look of the Tollund Man, life was harsh in ancient Denmark. Warfare was a constant problem. Intricately fashioned weapons have been recovered from burial sites.

TRAVEL BY SEA

Travel across the water was often easier and safer than going inland, where unknown dangers and fierce enemies lurked. So Danish shipbuilding evolved into an art. The first longboats were easily steered. They held a crew of forty-five and had plenty of storage space. Husky oarsmen and a single sail provided the energy that moved these fast boats. Each rower sat on a sea trunk that held his extra clothing.

The Viking Ship Hall at Roskilde displays the remains of several warships. Restoration of these sturdy vessels is continuing

A display at the Viking Ship Museum

under the watchful eye of the Institute of Marine Archaeology of the Danish National Museum.

FASCINATING DANISH VIKINGS

In Scandinavian languages, bays are called *viks*, so the bay people were called Vikings. These tough Danish seafarers eventually joined with their distant Scandinavian relatives to explore, pillage, and conquer. Remarkable artisans, their weapons were decorated with designs of elaborately entwined animals. One Viking design was called the "gripping beast." This was a four-footed smiling monster holding its left wrist with its right paw and its neck by a rear paw. These were usually found on the typical Viking weapon, a huge ax often inlaid with silver.

Ranging across the North Sea as early as A.D. 500, the Vikings poked and prodded the coasts of Britain and western Europe.

They went deep into Poland, Russia, and the Baltic lands. Some Vikings even made their way south into the Mediterranean Sea. Norwegian Vikings settled on the Atlantic islands and in Scotland and Ireland. Swedish Vikings made their way toward the Black Sea. The Danes overran northern Germany and invaded England.

The Anglo-Saxon king of Wessex in Britain was so afraid of the Danes that he gave them the *Danelaw,* a vast strip of rich land running from London to Chester. He was willing to do almost anything to keep the Danes from taking his entire country. Subsequently kings were forced to pay *danegeld,* enormous bribes of silver and gold. But the more they gave, the more the Vikings demanded.

Viking culture was extremely advanced. Well-designed villages and fortifications, marvelous artworks, progressive agricultural methods, and a well-developed political system with a parliament were important aspects of Viking life.

The Danish Vikings lived by a strict social code. They were hospitable to their friends. A guest would be offered a bath and the best place to sleep in the house to make him feel at home. There were many unwritten rules about conduct. Danish Vikings were not supposed to refuse a drink of mead, a sweet beer. But no one was supposed to drink too much. It was important always to tell the truth. Old people were highly respected and loyalty to friends was important. The Danes were careful to live up to all these courtly expectations.

DANISH GODS AND CHRISTIANITY

Originally the Danes, like the other Vikings, were pagans. Led by Odin, the Viking deities were generally considered to be loud

Artists' conceptions of Thor (left) and Odin (right)

and boisterous. Thor was Odin's son and was always depicted carrying a mighty hammer. He slammed around the heavens in a terrible temper and caused fierce thunderstorms, much to the dismay of his neighboring gods. A typical Viking warrior, called a *thegner* or *dreng*, would wear a miniature hammer around his neck to remind him that mighty Thor was his battlefield friend.

It was believed that Vikings who were killed in battle would be taken to Odin's court at *Valhalla*, the Hall of the Slain. According to legend, beautiful warrior maidens called Valkyries lifted the dead warriors by their hair and carried them into the afterlife.

Viking contact with other cultures slowly and subtly changed their lives. After a while, instead of burning Christian churches, the Vikings began attending services. One Danish Viking, King Harald Bluetooth, supported the introduction of Christianity into his country. Stone carvings dating from 985 tell how he encouraged his rowdy companions to be baptized.

Christianity brought many changes to Denmark. Almost

eighteen hundred of Denmark's nearly two thousand churches were built between 1100 and 1250, as Christianity steadily gained influence.

Farmers became estate owners. At local *moots,* "meetings," they came together to discuss crops, battles, and the latest gossip. The farmers objected to the growing central power of the king, usually the strongest warrior who had the best-trained men. On the other hand, growing towns challenged the authority of the local landowners.

The expanding influence of North German princes and commercial centers such as the great city of Lubeck (near present-day Hamburg, Germany) also were a constant problem. Under the first of the Valdemar line of kings, the Danes fought fierce battles with these unfriendly neighbors. Danish traders led by the kings wanted a greater influence in the Baltic and were willing to fight anyone for that privilege.

Legend says that the national flag, the *Dannebrog,* was dropped from heaven on June 15, 1219. This "miracle" turned defeat into victory against the Estonians at the Battle of Lindanaes. Actually, the red and white flag was probably given to Danish crusaders by a Catholic pope for their war against the pagans living along the eastern Baltic coast. Denmark and the other northern countries all adopted the same Christian cross as part of their flags, using different colors for different countries.

Not all battles were as successful. Despite his name, Valdemar the Victorious was captured and held for ransom by the Germans. This Valdemar, however, was also noted for the help he gave his country. He instituted a law code and established Denmark's first census.

KINGS OF DENMARK

Land-owning aristocratic families, however, weren't always so keen on the military adventures, especially because taxes were levied to pay for the wars. They preferred to keep their sons and their money at home. In 1282 they forced the king to sign the *Handfaestning*, "The Great Charter," establishing an annual parliament, the *Rigsdag*, to control the monarch's power. This was the first Danish constitution.

This turmoil enabled the landowning nobles of the neighboring German province of Holstein to extend their territory deep into Denmark. But the Danes were not good subjects. They constantly harassed the occupiers until they finally regained their freedom.

Under Valdemar IV, Denmark again became a mighty power of the northern seas. The new Danish empire extended to Norway and Sweden through marriages and inheritance of land. Valdemar died in 1375 without any heirs, so his daughter Margrete, who had married Haakon VI of Norway, ruled as regent for her son Olaf II. After Olaf died, his mother became queen of both Norway and Denmark in her own right. With Norway under Danish rule, the Faeroe Islands, Iceland, Sweden, and Greenland, as well as large parts of Finland were folded into the Danish cloak in the Kalmar Union. After Margrete I came the great-grandson of Valdemar IV at the end of the fourteenth century. This was Erik of Pomerania, who was elected king.

Christian II, who began his reign in 1513, is generally considered the first modern king of Denmark. His fierce subjugation of the Swedes led to a rebellion that lasted seven years. Christian eventually lost control of Sweden and the Kalmar Union ended. The Danish nobility hated him, and nicknamed him

Christian II, the Tyrant

Christian the Tyrant. That was from their perspective, because he enacted laws that favored the common people rather than themselves. During his heavy-handed reign, a civil war erupted, in which the wealthy landowners were pitted against the king. After losing most of his power to the rich nobles, Christian was exiled and eventually imprisoned in castles at Sonderborg and at Kalundburg, where he died in 1559.

By now the Protestant Reformation was sweeping Europe. The Roman Catholic church in the Scandinavian countries of Denmark, Sweden, and Norway crumbled under protests by reformers, who objected to the economic and political influence of the old church. The rulers of Denmark were jealous of the power exerted by the

Catholic archbishop. They also wanted to control the vast church estates, which made up about one-third of the country.

Under Christian III, Denmark finally became fully Protestant. The Lutheran faith was made the state religion.

Denmark was eventually swept into the horrors of the Thirty Years War, which lasted from 1618 to 1648. The war was fought over religion, money, territory, and power. Every nation that became involved had its own reasons for doing so. It was a bitter time for the ordinary people of Europe. Denmark was led by Christian IV, who wanted to protect the Protestant interests from those of the Catholics.

To finance his armies, Christian founded the Danish East and West Indies trading companies. He then modernized his navy. But he was no match for more powerful enemies. At the end of the long war, the Danish state was bankrupt. The countryside was ruined. No one was left to challenge the rise of the next powerful Danish ruler.

So Frederik III bribed the Rigsdag to give him power and make him absolute monarch. Frederik declared that his descendants would be Denmark's rulers forever. This effectively ended the elected monarchy. No one was brave enough to argue the point.

Frederik was a brilliant military tactician. He built many forts and strengthened the royal army. He had a cultured side as well, laying the foundation for the Danish museum system. Drawings of his elaborate crown are still used as official symbols of the Danish monarchy.

So Denmark moved into a new era, led by a hereditary line of kings that continues to today.

Chapter 3

THE KINGDOM GROWS

With Frederik III in total control of Denmark, the country's government actually functioned more smoothly. His centralized authority finally broke the power of the rich provincial families. During his reign from 1648 to 1670 Frederik's administration was extremely busy making laws. He polished his military tactics and kept a wary eye on competitors for the crown.

The king instituted a unified legal system, established schools, and developed an extensive network of roads. He even set up a standardized system of weights and currency that was the same throughout the kingdom.

All this contributed to a growing sense of national unity. They were the first steps toward making Denmark a modern society.

Like his ancestors, Frederik feared that the Swedes would eventually control the lucrative Baltic trade. When the king of Sweden was fighting in Poland, Frederik attacked him from behind. But Frederik lost the Danish-Swedish War.

LOSS OF THE PROVINCES

The treaties of Roskilde and Copenhagen gave Denmark's southern provinces, a portion of Norway, and several strategic islands to Sweden. Christian V, one of Frederik's sons, attempted to regain Denmark's lost territories during his reign.

This time, the country's military performed better. The Danish navy was excellent, reminiscent of the old Viking days. Niels Juel, a great Danish admiral, defeated the fleets of Sweden and its allies at the Battle of Oland on June 1, 1676. Juel won another victory in Koge Bay the next year.

Yet the victories did not stem the growing power of Sweden. Other Danish kings feebly attempted to retain what remained of their country's prestige. Yet some good resulted from this decline in international power. Over the next few decades, Denmark's rulers turned to matters at home. They concentrated on keeping the local populace happy. The kings gave more rights to the small landowners, improved the transportation system, and constructed many public buildings.

Throughout the late eighteenth and early nineteenth centuries, the Danes demonstrated their social concerns. In 1792 the nation became the first European country to ban slavery in its overseas possessions.

The French Revolution in 1789, which toppled kings and gave more power to the common man, at first had little effect on Denmark. Elsewhere the old monarchies were losing power and kings were losing their heads. Denmark kept to itself as the fury of rebellion swept Europe. Because of the turmoil, however, construction of battleships slowed down everywhere else on the continent. The clever Danes quickly stepped into this vacuum, offering their shipbuilding skills to anyone who would pay. In one year, sixty huge gunships were built in the Copenhagen shipyards.

The British bombarded Copenhagen in 1807.

BRITISH ATTACK

Denmark, however, could not keep out of the turmoil following the French Revolution. Denmark's geographic position was considered too important not to be coveted by other countries seeking prestige and power. The British feared that the Danes might ally themselves with Britain's enemies. They were angry that Denmark had signed an alliance with several countries that objected to the British searching their vessels on the high sea. In 1801 Copenhagen was bombarded by a British fleet led by the famous English admiral Horatio Nelson. The British almost destroyed the Danish capital.

In 1807 mighty French armies were rolling across Europe, gobbling up territory. The nervous Danes realized they had to choose between two strong opponents. The Danes cast their lot

Napoleon Bonaparte

with the French, led by Napoleon Bonaparte. That was an awful mistake, one that they were soon to regret.

In retaliation for this alliance, the powerful British navy again attacked Denmark, destroying or capturing most of the Danish navy. This catastrophe was disastrous for the little nation. The country was bankrupt by 1813, because the loss of its fleet meant economic ruin. In the following year, Danish King Frederik VI was forced to make peace with Britain and its Swedish and Russian allies. Norway was ceded to Sweden in the second great division of the old Danish empire.

With Norway lost, the Danes feared that their two largest southern provinces of Schleswig and Holstein would soon want to break away. They were correct. By the 1830s, nationalists were arguing that the two districts should be reunited with the German states. The parliament was divided between pro-Danish and pro-German forces. To further complicate the problem, a new constitution was drawn up in 1848 that forced King Frederik VII

The war between Denmark and Prussia in 1864

to give more power to the Rigsdag. The absolute monarchy
ended.

In addition, the Danish language and constitution were imposed
on Schleswig and Holstein's German-speaking citizens. The
Germans hated the new rules and took to the streets in a violent
revolution in 1849. Prussia, one of the strongest German states,
came to the Germans' assistance and invaded Jutland. After heavy
fighting, the Prussians eventually withdrew, but the ethnic and
political differences still festered.

WAR WITH THE PRUSSIANS

Under King Christian IX, a war broke out between Denmark
and Prussia, one of the German states that was allied with
Austria. This time, the outnumbered and outgunned Danes were
crushed by a wave of German bayonets at the Battle of Dybbol in
1864. Although they hoped for the best while suing for peace, the

peace of Vienna forced the Danes to give up the two southern provinces of Schleswig and Holstein.

This cut off almost a third of Denmark, along with more than 200,000 ethnic Danes who lived there. From 1871, when Germany became unified, these lands were considered part of the German empire.

Yet the loss was not as bad as it first appeared. Peace finally came to a war-ravaged Denmark. An astonishing economic recovery followed. Schools were improved. Farmers formed agricultural cooperatives and increased their yields by up-to-date cultivating methods. Dairy farming became important. Improved methods of separating cream from milk led to high-quality products. Danish butter was considered to be the best in the world.

Danes became more conscious of their environment. Wise leaders and concerned citizens knew they had to protect their countryside. They were among the first Europeans to launch major projects to renew the landscape.

In one of the most important undertakings, Enrico Dalgas organized the Danish Heath Society. This hard-working organization turned 247,000 acres (99,958 hectares) of barren heath into forestland for timber production. To improve trade with Britain, a new seaport, Esbjerg, was constructed on the west coast of Jutland in 1868.

These were golden years for political reforms. The power of the parliament outpaced that of the king. Denmark became truly a democratic monarchy. In 1901 King Christian IX appointed a new government and instituted numerous domestic reforms as more people moved from the country into the cities. In 1915 women were given the right to vote.

During the reign of King Christian IX, women were given the right to vote.

In World War I Denmark declared itself neutral, although Germany laid powerful mines in the rough seas around the Danish peninsula and disrupted trade. The farmers' cooperatives, however, helped the nation make it through those troubled times. Their excellent cultivation methods kept plenty of food on everyone's table until the war ended in 1918. The German empire and its allies were defeated.

After the war, pro-Danish residents of Schleswig demanded a vote to return to Denmark. The subdued Germany was too weak to argue. Subsequently, residents in about one-third of Schleswig voted to come back to Danish authority. By 1920 the nation's current borders were finally established.

A crowd of unemployed citizens demonstrated in front of the Folketing on February 25, 1932.

THE GREAT DEPRESSION

In the late 1920s and early 1930s, Denmark was badly hurt during the Great Depression, an economic collapse that caused financial ruin around the world. Money was almost worthless. Banks failed. Businesses collapsed. In 1933 Denmark's political parties agreed on emergency measures to help their people.

The burden of the country's debt was reduced. Farm prices were guaranteed. Trade controls were introduced and other measures undertaken to prop up the failing economy. By the end of the 1930s these quick actions helped reverse the slide.

But other crises loomed. The rise of Adolf Hitler's Nazi dictatorship in Germany was viewed with alarm by the Danes.

German soldiers marched in the streets of Copenhagen in 1940.

They remembered the military attacks by previous German rulers. Early in 1939 Denmark was forced to sign a nonaggression pact with Hitler. This treaty didn't mean much when Hitler launched World War II. He invaded Poland at the end of the year and sent his troops into Denmark without warning on April 9, 1940.

However, most of the Danish merchant fleet escaped the Germans. Skillful captains and crews helped the Allied forces throughout the remainder of the war. Although the Germans occupied Denmark, they were not supported by the populace. The Germans wanted to round up the Jews of Denmark and take them to concentration camps, as they did in other countries they overran. When the Nazis demanded all Jews wear arm bands to identify themselves, the king put an arm band on also. Then more and more Danes did likewise and the real Jews could not be identified.

WORLD WAR II

During the occupation, Danes helped thousands of Jewish citizens escape to neutral Sweden and carefully looked after their businesses and homes until the end of the war. The city of Copenhagen took the holiest of the Jewish religious writings, the *Torah*, and hid it in the basement of a church.

The Germans were furious because the Danes would not help them. In retaliation, they arrested and killed many political leaders, policemen, and teachers. Yet the courageous Danes continued to challenge the angry enemy. The level-headed, tolerant Danes often remarked that they didn't like people who shouted, especially the Germans.

The Danes resisted in many other ways. Basically, they ignored the German occupiers. They acted as if the Germans didn't exist. No one spoke to the occupiers. Other Danes wore woven caps that contained the colors of the Royal Air Force. The Danish underground resistance was formidable. A group of Jutland schoolboys called themselves the Churchill Club, named after the wartime prime minister of Great Britain. They blew up trains and attacked guard posts.

Marius Jensen was a Danish hero, captured by the Germans while scouting out one of their secret weather outposts on Greenland. He escaped by overpowering his captors and spent three weeks traveling by dog sled to safety. Jensen did not come back alone. He brought back the commander of the German weather station as his prisoner.

The Freedom Council, Denmark's underground government, secretly aided anti-German officials who remained in their jobs. After 1943 the Danish Cabinet resigned and the Council actually

In 1945 British troops were welcomed to Copenhagen.

governed the country despite the occupation. On May 5, 1945, the German troops surrendered, and battle-hardened British troops liberated Denmark several days later.

After the war, a coalition of political parties and resistance leaders set up a government. During these years, Liberal Democrats alternated power with the Conservatives, Social Democrats, and Radical Liberals. Political organizations such as the Socialist People's party also sprang up and gained several parliamentary seats. Everybody was glad for a political choice once again after years of repression. The few Danes who had aided the hated Germans were severely punished for their actions during the war.

Foreign Minister Gustav Rasmussen signs the treaty making Denmark part of NATO

REVISION OF THE CONSTITUTION

The Danish constitution was revised in 1953. The old upper chamber, the *Landsting,* was abolished, and a single chamber of parliament was introduced. All Danes had to work together as a team to help their country recover from the destruction of wartime.

As reconstruction proceeded quickly, the Danes took a respected place in world affairs. In 1949 they abandoned their neutrality and joined NATO–the North Atlantic Treaty Organization. NATO was formed during the Cold War to combat the growing power of the Soviet Union and its allies in the Warsaw Pact. The Danes felt more comfortable on the side of the Western, non-communist nations. They also eagerly joined the European Free Trade Association in 1959 and the European Community in 1973.

An SAS plane

Danes are proud members of the United Nations. Danish peace-keeping troops have been sent to the sun-scorched Middle East, the humid jungles of central Africa, the balmy Mediterranean island of Cyprus, and mountainous Kashmir. The Danes take their international responsibilities seriously.

Denmark was one of the first countries to sign and approve a ban on testing nuclear weapons. It also strongly opposed the manufacture of chemical and biological weapons. Young and old Danes have been active with the International Red Cross, the World Health Organization, and similar organizations that help the poor and helpless around the world.

Denmark and the other Scandinavian countries long ago put aside their differences. They work closely together on many projects. Shortly after World War II, Denmark, Norway, and Sweden decided to merge their national airlines into one. The resulting company was the Scandinavian Airlines System, more commonly known as SAS. The company now has a major office building in Copenhagen, which is truly the "Crossroads of Northern Europe."

Passports are no longer needed when citizens of one Scandinavian country visit another. A Swede can work in Norway, a Dane can have a job in Iceland, and a Finn can live in Denmark. Regardless of where each worker resides, he or she is entitled to the same medical care and social security, as well as numerous other benefits. With Denmark's approval of membership in the European Community, one passport will suffice throughout the twelve-country organization.

GOVERNMENT IN THE FAEROE ISLANDS AND GREENLAND

The Parliament of the Faeroe Islands, the *Lagting*, can trace its origins back at least one thousand years. In 1946 it voted for independence. There was much argument about whether this was a good idea. A new Parliament was elected and it reversed the independence decree. But the movement did not die and a compromise was reached. After negotiating with the central government, the Faeroe Islands received home rule. Under this system, they are still linked to Denmark and send two representatives to the *Folketing*, Denmark's Parliament.

Faeroe Island residents are considered Danish citizens. However, they have their own beautiful flag, a red cross outlined in blue on a white background. They also have their own banknotes and stamps.

The Faeroe Islanders administer their own industries, collect taxes, and dispense revenues. In the Danish administration, Faeroe Island affairs come under the control of the Danish prime minister, who appoints a high commissioner for the islands. The courts and police are directed by Denmark.

In 1933 the International Court of Justice in The Hague, the Netherlands, decreed that Greenland was officially part of Denmark. During World War II, when Denmark was controlled by the Germans, the United States took over the protection and supplying of the settlements on the islands. A new constitution was written for Greenland in 1953 that incorporated the island into the Danish kingdom on equal status with other territories. Since 1979 Greenland has had home rule like the Faeroe Islands, and it also sends two delegates to the Folketing. Greenland has generally followed a more independent economic course, as well.

THE SHARING SPIRIT

In 1971 the Scandinavian countries signed an agreement to share their cultural identity. A secretariat for cultural cooperation was headquartered in Copenhagen. Art and historical exhibits for galleries and museums, as well as folk musicians, symphonies, dance companies and other entertainment, and cultural groups now travel freely from one country to another. This has given rise to a strong spirit of cooperation. It enables the residents of each nation to understand the rich, and often similar, traditions of the others.

The Danes take a leading role in these cooperative efforts. They know that the world is shrinking and that friendly neighbors are extremely important.

Chapter 4

DENMARK'S LAND
OF DELIGHTS

Copenhagen

COPENHAGEN

It is easy for a visitor to fall in love with Denmark's capital. Golden church spires soar over the steep red tile rooftops. Smiling statues peek out from hidden corners. Museums and art galleries overflow with rare and wonderful treasures. Delightfully perfect parks are an important part of Copenhagen life. They are a place in which to play, rest tired feet, watch the passing crowd, sing songs, and meet friends. One of the most popular parks is named after H.C. Oersted, the discoverer of electromagnetism. The tiny square of green is wonderful, especially in the sunny springtime when the trees are freshly budding.

Ancient records first mention Copenhagen in 1034, although there were Danes living in the region centuries before. It occupies an especially strategic location. In the Danish tongue, the city name is spelled *København*, taken from the words *køben*, "merchant" and *havn*, "harbor." In 1254 Copenhagen received its royal charter and became the official capital of Denmark in 1536. The city of Copenhagen will celebrate its 830th anniversary in 1997.

The Borsen, the oldest stock exchange building in the world still

Opposite page: An aerial view of the city of Copenhagen and a closeup of the Borsen (bottom left), the oldest stock exchange still in use

in use (on special occasions only), and much of the rest of the old city was built between 1619 and 1640 during the reign of Christian IV. Called the architect king, Christian wanted to showcase his wonderful eye for design. His pet project, Copenhagen, is now one of the largest cities in Scandinavia.

Visitors hardly notice Copenhagen's crowds because the entire urban area is a delightful mix of bustling modern and elegant traditional. Despite the city's size, a Copenhagen resident can be at a seaside beach or on the way to a summer home quickly.

In any direction a casual stroller can find a dock or quay that captures the heady smells of salt and freshly caught herring. The creaking of sailboat masts, the rumble of barges, and the puff-puff of powerful tugboats emphasize the city's maritime heritage. Giant oceangoing freighters dock along the wharves near the cluttered, noisy Burmeister and Wain shipyards, Denmark's largest single industrial firm. These shipyards built the first oceangoing motor ship in the world in 1912, after purchasing the patent for the diesel engine from its inventor, Otto Diesel. All these boats are as much a part of Copenhagen as the autos and bicycles on the avenues.

For hundreds of years, fish have been sold in Gammelstrand. This was once a village that was absorbed into greater Copenhagen. The fish sellers are colorful characters, each one shouting that his or her fish are the best and the freshest in all Denmark.

Copenhagen has many canals and waterways. There is a vast square in front of the *Radhus*, "city hall." In the square, old men sun themselves on benches, flower sellers ply their trade, photographers snap pictures, and buses unload their passengers.

Roads and parks have replaced the walls that once surrounded

Opposite page: The large square in front of the city hall, which is the building with the clock tower The canals of Copenhagen are crowded with sailing ships (inset).

Part of Christiansborg Fortress (left) holds the Folketinget, *or Parliament House. The statue of the Little Mermaid (right)*

the heart of medieval Copenhagen, which lay on the east side of the island of Zealand. Today, *Vestervoldgade,* "Western Wall Street," Norregade, and Gothersgade form three sides of the city core. The fourth side is the harbor with the islands of Slotsholmen and Amager.

Christiansborg Fortress and the Supreme Court, the Ministry of Foreign Affairs, the Court Theater, and the Royal Library (which holds 125 million books) are on Slotsholmen. The wide lanes of the Langebro Bridge connect Amager with the rest of Copenhagen.

A winsome statue of the Little Mermaid, a character from a Hans Christian Andersen fairy tale, overlooks the harbor. The famous bronze sculpture was made by Edvard Eriksen in 1913. From her vantage point, she can keep a close watch over the oceangoing freighters, huffing tugboats, and graceful yachts.

Twinkling lights outline Tivoli at night. The main entrance (above right) is through a massive arch.

What was once a protective moat around Copenhagen is now a string of charming little parks and lakes, including the world-famous amusement park, Tivoli. The main entrance to Tivoli is through a massive arch, leading to a twenty-acre (eight-hectare) wonderland. At night Tivoli is lighted with thousands of twinkling lights. Open-air musical performances are held here on lazy summer afternoons. In the concert hall the orchestra gives free shows. Twenty-three restaurants serve everything from the famous Danish smorgasbord to full gourmet meals. Every Saturday and Sunday, the Tivoli Boy Guards march around the park, with drums thumping and trumpets blaring. Shooting galleries, a Hall of Mirrors, and spins on the Big Dipper and similar rides add to the fun. In the summer, midnight fireworks on Wednesday, Friday, and Saturday end the day with breathtaking explosions of sparkling color.

*Amalienborg (above) is the royal residence.
A statue of King Frederik V is in the square.
Christianhavn (right) is the artists'
section of Copenhagen.*

Copenhagen's "New Town" contains the elegant Amalienborg Palace complex where the queen lives. The palace actually consists of four separate buildings, each with different names. The royal family uses the upper story of the Schack Palace as their residence. The other buildings are used for offices, meetings, and houses for visiting dignitaries. It is easy to know whenever the queen is at home. When she is there, the royal guard changes daily at noon.

One of the most colorful sections of the city is Christianhavn. This quaint old section of town is the artists' quarter, packed with street musicians, shops, museums, small hotels, and dozens of tiny restaurants.

Picturesque Nyhavn

Nyhavn is along a canal in another often-visited section of Copenhagen. The blue-green waters there are fronted by narrow streets and gabled merchants' houses painted in bold pink, aqua, and yellow.

Stroget is the city's main shopping district, made up of several pedestrian malls with limited vehicle traffic winding through the Old City. Fancy shops and outdoor cafés cater to residents and visitors.

Copenhagen, northern Europe's largest city, lives up to its title as one of the most delightful cities in Europe.

*The port at Ålborg (left) and gravestones at
the Lindholm Hoje burial site (right)*

TWO GRADE "A" CITIES: ÅLBORG AND ÅRHUS

Ålborg is the fourth-largest city in Denmark, situated on the
south bank of the picturesque Lim Fjord. The city is an important
industrial center, with shipbuilding and cement manufacturing as
two of its most important businesses. From the modern port,
ships carry goods to far-off Greenland.

Not far from the city is the Lindholm Hoje burial site where
graves of 682 Viking warriors have been discovered. Rings of
stone mark the field where the bodies once lay. Remains of a
Viking settlement dating to the tenth century also have been
found. Many artifacts from the site are displayed in the Historical
Museum of Ålborg.

Dating from 928, Århus is Denmark's second-largest city. It lies

Views of Århus include the busy central section near the port (right) and an open-air museum (above).

on the east coast of Jutland and has a major harbor with five docks and a fishing harbor. A ferry service from the port connects the city to Zealand and to the outer islands that belong to Denmark.

Århus is another Danish city with wonderful museums. The Danish Fire Brigade Museum houses more than sixty old-fashioned vehicles, including those once pulled by horses. At the Århus Viking Museum, visitors can see a reconstruction of a rampart that once ringed the ancient town. The Moesgard Prehistoric Museum, about six miles (ten kilometers) south of Århus, is now home to the Grauballe Man. This is a perfectly preserved body of an ancient man dating back at least sixteen hundred years. Around the museum is a trail that leads past reconstructions of Stone Age and Bronze Age buildings.

Visitors to Lego Land can enjoy a miniature city (left) and a safari via railroad (above), complete with Lego giraffes.

THE BUILDING BLOCKS OF BILLUND

The little town of Billund in central Jutland has only seven thousand residents, but it is known for its major industry, Lego Land A/S. The factory produces Lego plastic bricks. *Lego* is actually the Latin word for "I read." But the inventor of Legos, Ole Kirk Christiansen, didn't use the word in the same sense. He composed the name of his toys from two Danish words: *leg* and *godt*, which means "play well." Christiansen was an unemployed cabinetmaker in the 1930s when he started making wooden blocks from which children could make their own toys. In the 1950s his company started using the famous plastic bricks that can be locked together.

Helsingor is a quiet town at the northeastern tip of Zealand.

In 1968 the company opened Lego Land, a theme park in which almost everything is made from Legos. Famous buildings from all over the world have been reconstructed in miniature. There is even an entire village made of Legos. Children can ride Lego cars on a Lego safari, looking at animals made from Legos.

HAMLET'S HELSINGOR

This old Danish port on Zealand is best known in its English spelling, "Elsinore." According to legend, this is where Prince Hamlet lived. He was a character in a famous William Shakespeare play. The town is only 3 miles (4.8 kilometers) from Sweden, and during World War II it was a gateway for refugees fleeing Denmark. The 39-foot (12-meter) Swedish Pillar stands in the town as a thank you to Denmark's neighbors who helped them during the German occupation.

*The Louisiana Museum (left) and a gallery of
modern art (right) inside the museum*

Helsingor is now known for its Danish Museum of Technology.
It holds just about everything imaginable, from entire trains to
airplanes. Six miles (ten kilometers) south of town is the Louisiana
Museum, one of Scandinavia's most famous modern art museums.
The facility was founded in 1958 by industrialist and art lover
Knud W. Jensen and overlooks a vast blue-green bay. The
Louisiana hosts special exhibitions, poetry readings, and concerts.

BEASTS AND BANDHOLM

Bandholm, on the island of Lolland in the Baltic Sea, is home to
the Knuthenborg Safari Park. Antelopes, zebras, giraffes, camels,
elephants, and even a rhinoceros roam on the 1,500-acre (607-
hectare) grounds of the largest manor house in Scandinavia. The

*A statue of Hans Christian Andersen stands (left)
in Odense. Egeskov Castle in Odense (right)*

enclave is surrounded by a five-mile (eight-kilometer) wall, to
make certain that none of the resident ostriches or monkeys
escape to bother the neighbors' cows. But a road leads through
the center of the park from which all the animals can be seen up
close. A special enclosure contains Bengal tigers.

ODENSE

Denmark's third-largest town is Odense on the island of Fyn.
This is an important industrial town, dating from at least 988. It is
believed that the site on which the town grew was once a Viking
holy place. Supposedly, the god Odin was worshiped here.

The most famous native son in residence here was the Danish
writer Hans Christian Andersen. In his honor the town made him

This little house in Odense is where Hans Christian Andersen lived with his parents when he was a young boy.

an honorary citizen and built the Hans Christian Andersen Museum. Its halls contain much of Andersen's furniture and many of his original manuscripts.

RELIGIOUS ROSKILDE

One of the most ancient towns in Denmark is Roskilde. Legend says that Harald Bluetooth, who converted the Danes to Christianity, built a wooden church here in 960. Over the ensuing centuries, Roskilde was a rich religious center.

During the Protestant Reformation in the sixteenth century, many of Roskilde's churches were closed and the city lost much of its importance. With the Treaty of Roskilde in 1658, peace was reached in a war between a defeated Denmark and victorious Sweden. Denmark gave up many of its island possessions and other territory to its powerful neighbor.

Many royal Danes are buried in Roskilde Cathedral (left). The Lejre Archaeological Research Center (above) where residents live, work, and dress as their ancestors did centuries ago.

Roskilde eventually became a factory city, with a modern atomic research center outside town. One of the most interesting places in this ancient town is the Viking Ship Museum.

Near the city is the Historico-Archaeological Research Center of Lejre, which depicts a typical Stone Age community. Danes and other visitors often spend holidays here, living as their ancestors. They use heavy wooden plows pulled by oxen to prepare the field, bake bread on hearths, and generally learn to live like a typical family from that long-ago era.

THE FAEROE ISLANDS

Sheep raising and fishing are the islanders' principal sources of income. Even the children help their parents tend the flocks or work the fishing boats. Chores are part of the regular day before and after school. Today, there are about forty-two thousand persons on the Faeroe Islands. The largest town, the capital of

The town and harbor of Torshavn in the Faeroe Islands

Torshavn, has about fourteen thousand citizens. The southernmost village is Sumba on the island of Sudhuroy. The northernmost is Vidareidi on Vidoy island.

CITIES OF GREENLAND

Most of the villages are on the southern and middle portion of Greenland's western coast. The capital and largest town of Greenland is called Nuuk in the local language and Godthab in Danish. The city has a population of more than eleven thousand.

*Nuuk, the capital of Greenland (above), and a closeup
of a totem pole from the coast of Greenland (inset)*

It is situated on a chilly fjord that cuts deeply into the west coast
of the island. Two museums in the city show interesting artifacts
from Eskimo life and art.

In World War II Greenland was a valuable listening post for the
Allies who spied on German submarines. In 1990 an expedition
found several Allied fighters and bombers that had made
emergency landings on the island's glaciers. By the time they
were discovered, some of the planes were buried deep in the ice,
as mush as 250 feet (76 meters). The first plane to be discovered
was sent as a gift to the Danish government.

Nuuk

Chapter 5

DOINGS IN DENMARK

Denmark has fewer natural resources than many nations. But it is not at a trade disadvantage. The Danes pay for their imported raw materials by exporting finished products at a profit. The Danes have always relished this challenging economic juggling act. By hard work and providing high-quality goods needed by other countries, Denmark has developed a favorable balance between imports and exports. The country has one of the highest standards of living in the world.

Denmark has many other advantages. Its banks have extensive international experience. The Danes can look back at a long mercantile trade, one that started before the Viking age. They have a proud heritage of being businesspeople who know how to strike good deals.

Today, Denmark belongs to the European Community (EC). This alliance peacefully and profitably strengthens Denmark's commercial ties with other countries. Danes appreciate the value of understanding how other cultures think and act. Most successful Danish businesspeople speak fluent English and German. This ability to communicate is necessary in the highly competitive business world. Knowledge of Japanese is becoming another asset, as Asia is brought into the Danish marketplace.

Germany, Sweden, and Great Britain are among Denmark's best trading partners. Yet the country's goods and expertise can pop up anywhere. Danish companies provided construction materials for a modern automobile plant in Brazil. Its engineers designed a towering grain elevator in Turkey. Sleek Danish-built sailboats and massive supertankers sail under the flags of many countries. Danish-built research equipment has even landed on the moon!

Other factors help Denmark pump up its economic muscle. First, the country is small. It is easy to get around in Denmark because of its highly efficient network of roads, ports, air terminals, ferryboats, and rail lines. This enhances Denmark's reputation in what is a critical international marketplace. Since Danish companies can produce goods quickly, shipping commodities from factories to the world's store shelves is fast and efficient. Danes don't like to waste time. They are noted for punctual deliveries and standing behind their products.

Danish firms strongly favor the latest in technology. For years, Denmark was a successful agricultural country, but gradually expanded its industrial base after World War II. Consequently, most Danish factories are relatively new and the equipment is regularly updated.

The Danes are shrewd. They know that they cannot compete on all levels of business with other industrial nations. So they look for niches where they can make a difference. For instance, Denmark capitalized on its long love affair with the sea and has

Most of the world's hearing aids are made in Denmark.

become a leading manufacturer of modern marine diesel engines. In addition, it produces 30 percent of the world's cement and most of the world's hearing aids, controls for thermostats, and industrial enzymes.

Danish researchers are skilled at finding techniques to produce their goods faster and better. More than half of the country's workers are in companies with fewer than two hundred employees. So it is generally an easy process to introduce manufacturing innovations. Workers do not have to struggle past many layers of management to arrive at decisions that help customers. Large and small companies encourage employee involvement, creativity, and risk-taking.

In addition, Danish firms consider it their responsibility to become involved in community affairs. The Carlsberg Brewery donates large amounts of its profits to the arts world and doesn't

The whimsically painted Tuborg beer company

forget to support chemical and biological research. The management at the Tuborg Brewery supports a foundation that awards important grants for scientific and agricultural study, the production of handicrafts, and industrial expansion.

There are about six thousand companies in Denmark. Most are privately owned. The postal service and most transportation systems are publicly managed. Although the government has never stepped in to run a company, the public and private sectors cooperate closely. State-owned institutions sometimes combine with private firms to form a corporation.

Copenhagen is the industrial heart of Denmark and home to most of the nation's manufacturing plants. The city has a large automobile production plant and is noted for manufacture of excellent porcelain and furniture.

The birdhouse on this farmstead looks just like a miniature farm building.

DOWN ON THE FARM

Today, fewer than 8 percent of Danes still work on farms. This has been a relatively recent development. In fact, it was not until 1958 that industry exported more goods than did the agricultural sector. But once manufacturing took off, the move away from farming was rapid.

This does not mean that agriculture has taken a back seat in Denmark. Far from it. Danes have pioneered animal breeding and crop cultivation techniques that have helped farmers around the world. Delicious Danish ham and excellent cheese and other dairy products remain valuable exports. Rigid controls and constant inspections guarantee quality.

The average Danish farm is between 25 and 75 acres (10 and 30 hectares). Growing of vegetables is a mainstay of the Danish

Cheese from dairy cattle (top left) and ham from pigs (left) are exported. Potatoes (above) are fed to pigs or made into alcohol or flour for industrial use.

agricultural scene. Tons of carrots, onions, cabbages, and sugar beets are produced each year on the outer islands and shipped to processing centers. The soil and weather conditions are more favorable on the islands. Potatoes and turnips are principal crops in western Jutland. The potatoes are fed to pigs or made into alcohol or flour for industrial use.

Cattle seem to be everywhere in Jutland. Danish breeds are noted for their high milk production.

Producer cooperatives carefully inspect, grade, and market high-quality farm products. Agricultural scientists have perfected many innovations, including a "streamlined" pig that has less fat.

GETTING GOODS AROUND

The railroad network totals about 17,820 miles (28,678 kilometers) and is supervised by the Danish State Railways. The

A Falck vehicle tows a disabled car (above). The Danish State Railways own their own ferry system (inset).

railway system even owns its own ferry lines and several ships. The freighters, tankers, and liners of the privately owned Danish merchant fleet sail the world's oceans.

The state highway system consists of almost 3,000 miles (4,828 kilometers) of main roads, in addition to 33,000 miles (53,107 kilometers) of secondary roads. A freeway system is not hampered by the fjords and inlets separating many of the Danish islands. Tunnels, bridges, and ferries provide safe, efficient connections. The word *Falck* is painted on the sides of trucks often seen along the highways. These are emergency vehicles. The drivers offer assistance to motorists in trouble.

Kastrup, about six miles (ten kilometers) from Copenhagen, is one of Denmark's urban centers and home of a major international airport. It only takes about seventy-five minutes to fly to Amsterdam from Copenhagen, eight hours and forty minutes to New York, and seventeen hours to Tokyo (via the North Pole).

A variety of ships are seen in Denmark's ports.

SAS has a beautiful twenty-two-story office and hotel in central Copenhagen. The imposing tower was designed by Arne Jacobsen. Its modern glass and concrete lines are different from the capital's more traditional buildings.

Copenhagen's harbor is an exotic blend of ships from dozens of countries. Tankers, freighters, refrigerator vessels, tugs, pilot boats, and other craft come and go across the blue-brown waters to the docks and terminals. More than thirty-five thousand ships pass through the port each year.

Other major Danish ports are located in Århus, Ålborg, Esbjerg, Odense, and Ronne. There are smaller commercial docks and privately owned harbors scattered along the seacoast. Many are owned by multinational oil companies such as Esso, Shell, and Gulf. Their huge supertankers, each as long as several city blocks, dock here after lengthy voyages from the Middle East where much of the oil is produced.

SOCIAL AND WORKING CONDITIONS

Danish workers average a forty-hour week but are willing to put in extra time if necessary. There is equal pay for both men and women in the same jobs, a legal requirement since 1973.

The Danish Sex Discrimination Act even prohibits advertising for workers of only one sex. Women's rights are nothing new in Denmark. Author Thomasine Gyllembourg, who lived from 1773 to 1856, demanded the right to education, to vote, and to run for office for women, even those who were unmarried. The Danish Women Citizen's Society was formed in 1871 to support significant issues such as allowing women to work outside the home. Its magazine, *Kvinden og Samfundet*, *"Women and Society,"* is still being published.

Other women's organizations keep a close watch on the status of their members and women in general. An association of housewives, the *Husmoderforeninger*, is as active as professional white-collar groups.

Equality did not come easily. In the 1970s, a woman's movement called "Redstockings" launched a series of protests. Wearing bright red hose, women marched through cities around Denmark. They emphasized that because women as well as men were human beings, they were entitled to the same economic rights as men. The Joan Sisters were another group of activists who sought improved respect for women. They set up day care centers for working parents and actively supported women candidates who ran for political office.

Danish workers receive an average of five weeks' paid vacation every year. Mothers and fathers can qualify for fourteen weeks of maternity leave with pay to take care of their newborns.

Elderly Danes receive pensions from the state.

Government-operated and private nurseries and day-care centers are available for children after their parents return to work. Because of the strong health care system, there is an extremely low infant mortality rate in Denmark.

Sometimes individuals lose their jobs, as often happens with seasonal construction workers. Unemployment benefits paid can amount to as much as 90 percent of weekly earnings for a specified period of time.

From the age of sixty-seven years (from fifty-five years for widows), each Danish citizen receives a pension from the state. As an increasing percentage of Danes are living longer, more care has been taken to accommodate their needs. Currently, the average life expectancy is around seventy-one years. Many elderly Danes live in collective housing, where they remain in the community but have a special communication link with a nearby hospital or care facility. Others are in sheltered housing that offers more on-site medical and social assistance. Full-care housing has been built for the elderly and the handicapped. These institutions can be private or operated by the local government.

Taxes are high in Denmark, but they pay for essential services to make life easier, such as complete medical and hospital care as well as education. A Danish worker may pay as much as 54 percent income and 22 percent sales taxes to cover the cost of the extensive social service network. The government spends 45 percent of its budget on this welfare system, which is high compared with that of other nations. Another 12 percent is spent on education and only 7 percent on military and defense.

If a citizen wants to complain about taxes or discuss any other pertinent subject, he or she has the right to talk with a cabinet minister. From 10:00 to 11:00 each Thursday morning the ministers hold an open house. Ordinary Danes can drop by for a chat, a complaint, or a request for help. If a cabinet minister is not going to be present for one of these sessions, public notice must be given at least two days in advance.

The Danes even have a government ombudsman who considers citizen complaints against the government. The ombudsman's responsibility is to see that officials behave themselves and act responsibly. If the ombudsman learns of major mistakes or wrongdoing, he must report immediately to the Folketing and the appropriate minister. The first ombudsman was unanimously appointed in 1955.

Workers are well paid. They have extra money to purchase televisions, stereos, and video equipment and to take vacations. Almost 8 percent have summer cottages. Most people own cars. Homes and apartments are bright, comfortable, and spacious.

The Danish Federation of Trade Unions is the strongest labor group in the country. The federation is a consortium of about forty different unions, with almost a million members. The Joint Council of Danish Public Servants' and Salaried Employees'

Construction workers put a thatch roof on a house.

Organizations and the Central Organization of Civil Servants take care of the labor needs for many office and managerial workers. Even the employers have their own organization, the Danish Employers' Federation, which represents about twenty-one thousand employers.

The unions and government cooperate in supervising an excellent system of training for young people wishing to specialize. The trainees must spend four years in the construction trades, technological professions, and other skilled employment before they are fully qualified.

As Denmark strides into the future, government, management, and labor realize the importance of continually working together. They might not always agree on everything, but they know cooperation will keep their country economically strong and socially responsible. And the extensive welfare system ensures that there is little economic difference between Danes. That fact, say the citizens of this small country, is another measure of their humanity.

*Artists have always been
encouraged and their works,
from traditional (above) to ultra-modern
(left), can be seen everywhere.*

Chapter 6

A LAND OF
ARLS AND LETTERS

Danes pride themselves on their rich artistic heritage. They have a long history of public support for the arts. In the eighteenth and nineteenth centuries, the state donated large amounts of money to individual artists and writers. Even world-renowned figures such as storyteller Hans Christian Andersen and sculptor Bertel Thorvaldsen were among the many Danes who needed financial help in their careers.

Bringing culture to the people is important. Folk high schools were established in the nineteenth century to ensure that young Danes in rural areas had access to culture. The establishment of these schools coincided with the development of the Danish public library system.

In 1961 a ministry of cultural affairs was established to promote and encourage the country's creativity. A National Endowment for the Arts was set up in 1964 and updated in 1974. Large grants and awards are given each year to composers, filmmakers, sculptors, writers, and others. New works are commissioned, travel money is allocated, and lectures are established. Denmark takes its cultural responsibilities seriously.

Det Kongelige Teater

Promoting culture takes many forms. Even comic books have their place in schools as a fun way to teach reading. Danish Radio sponsors several programs aimed at young people. Libraries have quiet nooks for children where they can listen to records or read. Theater productions focus on young viewers. After all, who could resist laughing at *The Spinach Eater*, featuring Popeye and all his silly friends.

THEATER

Det Kongelige Teater, "The Royal Theater," in Copenhagen is run as a state institution. It presents a widely diversified schedule of drama, ballet, opera, and modern dance by contemporary as well as historic Danish figures. Actually the Royal Theater consists of two large halls and one small theater, plus touring companies. One of the touring companies presents productions for young people.

Everyone is excited when the Touring Children's Theater and Visiting Theater arrive. Plays and musical productions are staged in schools, town halls, and small theater buildings.

There are another twenty independent theaters in Copenhagen and numerous theater companies outside the capital. Seventy-two of these theaters are exclusively aimed at young people.

The Comedy Wagon, The Gang, The Umbrella Theater, and others have even taken the theater message to nursery schools and parks. Each year, a Children's Theater Festival is held near Copenhagen, where dozens of productions are staged.

Government-run regional theaters in Århus, Odense, and Ålborg emphasize local productions as well as providing a home away from home for the national touring companies.

To encourage theater attendance, the government has several plans that subsidize tickets. The government often pays the difference in price. All children and students under the age of twenty-five get their tickets at half price.

MUSIC

The first proof of music making in Denmark was the discovery in 797 of six wind instruments dating from the Bronze Age (1100-500 B.C.). These horns, called lurs, were found near Copenhagen and resembled the rustic forms used by shepherds. Bone flutes and gold horns dating from the same period have subsequently been discovered in ancient grave sites.

During the Middle Ages, church music and folk ballads were the principal musical forms. The Danish royal courts always had a composer or two on staff whose duties were to write scores for the entertainment of the king.

Tenor Lauritz Melchior

Carl Nielsen, son of a housepainter who was also an amateur fiddler, became one of his country's most beloved composers and conductors. As a youngster, Nielsen would often perform with his father at weddings and other local celebrations. At age eight he composed his first dance tunes. The family and neighbors encouraged Nielsen to rehearse. They would often gather at his house to hear him practice Mozart and Haydn compositions. With those skills carefully nurtured, he applied for an apprenticeship in a military band in Odense, a city near his home. He won the job at age fourteen and began his musical career in earnest.

Over his lifetime, Nielsen's works ranged from operas to full symphonies, many of which were introduced at Denmark's Royal Theater. Two of his most famous operas were *Saul and David* and *Masquerade.*

The first Danish-born musician to be successful abroad was organist Diderik Buxtehude, whose writing and reputation for

Pianist Victor Borge

performing grand compositions was unrivaled in the eighteenth century. He performed throughout Europe and was visited by Bach, Handel, and other great musicians who loved his performances. Throughout the years, other Danish organists have been received well at home and in other countries. Grethe Krogh Christensen became a professor at the Royal Danish Conservatory after a long award-winning career in the 1950s and 1960s.

Tenor Erik Schmedes found a home singing at the Vienna Opera in Austria and performed at the Metropolitan Opera in New York City. Another tenor, Lauritz Melchior, was the leading Wagnerian tenor at the Metropolitan from 1925 to 1950.

Danish pianists have been outstanding. Their skillful fingers have captured the charm and grace of contemporary and traditional composers from many lands. The best known is Victor Borge, a concert pianist turned musical comedian, who has amused audiences for years with his "impossible" playing.

A rock festival in Roskilde

Not all music in Denmark is in the classical vein. Folk, jazz, and contemporary music are just as popular here as in other countries. Concert halls are always filled with visiting entertainers, demonstrating that music of all kinds remains a special part of Danish life.

WRITERS

Of all the Danish writers, the most famous is probably Hans Christian Andersen. The story of his life reads like one of his fairy tales. Andersen, the son of a shoemaker, munched chocolates with kings and queens after he grew up. He never married but was close friends with many important women of Europe. He never had a home of his own. He lived with friends or in hotel rooms. He often was lonely, yet everywhere he went he was surrounded by admirers.

Hans Christian Andersen

Andersen often likened himself to the character in one of his most famous tales, *The Ugly Duckling*. The tall, skinny author had a craggy face with a large nose. His large hands seemed too big for the rest of his body.

Andersen traveled abroad at least twenty-nine times. Some of his trips took several months, going by train, on the back of donkeys, or by stagecoach. Andersen always carried a long rope in his trunk wherever he went. He figured the rope would help him escape a building in case of fire. Yet his fears never interfered with his interest in what was going on around him. He attended the opera in Paris, visited a harem in Constantinople, and was caught in a flood in Spain. All these adventures contributed to his storytelling charm. His writings are rich with details.

Andersen became the world's storyteller. *The Emperor's New Clothes*, *The Red Shoes*, *The Tinder Box*, *The Ugly Duckling*, and his other works have been translated into many languages. Although

Søren Kierkegaard (left) and Baroness Karen Blixen (right)

he never visited the United States, a statue of the famed author is a popular gathering spot in New York City's Central Park.

Another major voice in Danish literature is that of philosopher and theologian Søren Aabye Kierkegaard. His writings are dark and brooding. He wrote about his deep personal relationship with God but did not have any use for organized religion. Critics made fun of Kierkegaard and mocked his views. It wasn't until a hundred years after his death that he was finally recognized as a genius. His most famous works include *Repetition* and *Either/Or*, both written in 1843, and *Stages on Life's Way*, written in 1845.

Baroness Karen Blixen was one of Denmark's most famous women writers. She was an industrious coffee farmer who lived in East Africa (now Kenya) in the 1920s. Her memoirs of those days, *Out of Africa*, formed the basis for an award-winning movie of the same name starring Robert Redford and Meryl Streep. Under her pen name of Isak Dinesen, Blixen wrote a series of intriguing stories called *Seven Gothic Tales*. During the German occupation of Denmark, she used the name Pierre Andrezel to write many features that indirectly criticized the invaders.

On Kenya's independence day in December 1963, Blixen presented her farmhouse to the new nation. It is now used as a training center for young African women.

Martin Anderson Nexö is remembered for his works advocating socialism, especially *Pelle the Conqueror*.

Greenlanders have a rich literary heritage. The Greenland Publishing Company issues between fifty and one hundred new books each year in the Greenlandic language. The local printing company has been operating for more than one hundred years.

FILMS

Denmark was one of the first Scandinavian countries to produce high quality movies. In December 1896, only a few months after the first motion pictures were being exhibited in Paris, several short documentary movies were being made in Denmark. They were made by Peter Elfelt, who would eventually become photographer for the Royal Court. He also photographed the country's first fiction film, *The Execution*, in 1903.

In 1904, Denmark's first permanent movie house opened in Copenhagen. The Kosmorama was typical of the elaborate theaters of the day, featuring silent movies produced by Europe's best artists.

Danish filmmakers are noted for their honesty. Henning Carlsen directed many critically acclaimed movies, including *Old People*, *Dilemma*, and *The Cats*. Each story focused on the problems of life in Scandinavia. One of his better-known works is a comedy, *To Be on the Bandwagon!* that depicts the down-and-out customers who hung out at The Ostrich Café.

The Danish sense of humor comes out strongly in many movies. Kirsten Stenbaek has made several successful comedies, including *The Dreamers*, *The Mad Dane*, and *Lenin, You Rascal*. Erik Balling produced a comedy series focusing on what he called "The Olsen Gang," a trio of bumbling friends who always seem to get in and out of trouble. *The Olsen Gang's Big Haul* and the *Olsen Gang in Jutland* are typical of Balling's rollicking movies.

This heritage of fine filmmaking in Denmark has long had the support of the Danish government. A Government Film Office was set up in 1939 to purchase and distribute documentary and educational movies. In 1965, the Danish Film Foundation was established to actively promote the art of moviemaking.

A Children's Film Council, a joint project of the film institute and government film office, recommends awarding of grants to producers who make films for young people.

About twenty-five films are still produced each year in Denmark, keeping alive the spirit of an art form that started almost a century ago. Two Danish movies have received Oscars as best foreign movies of the year from the Academy of Motion Picture Arts and Sciences in the United States. The first, for a film version of author Karen Blixen's *Babette's Feast*, won in 1988, and the second went to an adaptation of Nexö's *Pelle the Conqueror* in 1989.

DANCE

Of all the dance forms in Denmark, ballet is one of the oldest and most distinguished. As early as 1722, ballet was an integral part of court performances. At first, ballet masters and choreographers from Italy and France taught the courses and devised the productions. That was all right with the Danes. They were always ready with open arms to greet anyone who could dance well.

ARTISTS

There are many artists from Denmark, but few have gained fame elsewhere. One who is well known is Bertel Thorvaldsen, a sculptor who specialized in the Greek style of lifelike creations. Thorvaldsen's sculptures are usually in white marble and include monuments and portrait busts.

ARTS AND COMMUNICATION IN THE FAEROE ISLANDS

Although the Faeroe Islands seem isolated, they are linked to the mainland by ferryboat and airplane and have an active cultural life. There is a professional drama company in Torshavn, and numerous amateur acting troupes are scattered through the villages. Most towns have a film theater, as well as choral groups and orchestras. Seven newspapers are published on the islands, five of which are tied to political parties. Local radio and television keep the islands up to date on the latest news, and signals from Denmark, Norway, and other European nations can be picked up.

Although they wrote in Danish, eventually such twentieth-century Faeroese writers as Jorgen-Frantz Jacobsen and William Heinesen received international acclaim.

Chapter 7

THE WONDERFUL STATE
OF THE DANES

With its strategic location at the junction of the northern oceans, Denmark has been called a crossroads for new ideas. Danes generally have a tolerant, open-minded attitude. Ideas and new ways of doing things come not only from visitors but also from travel-loving Danes. The best of everything is then folded into the Danish way of life.

Because of Denmark's small size, each citizen is important. No one gets lost in the crowd. The Danish government is concerned that everyone be treated equally and fairly. Citizens look out for each other.

The Danes are practical, inventive, and adapt easily to almost every situation. There is a keen artistic sense in Denmark, one that molds basic ideas into special results. Good taste is demonstrated in the clean lines of handcrafted Danish Modern

Opposite page: A pedestrian area in downtown Copenhagen

Modern furniture (left) and pottery and glassware (right)

furniture and the trim shapes of teapots, as well as in the muscular angles of heavy manufactured goods. Every year the Danish Society for Industrial Design gives an award for outstanding achievement in product design and development. Danish textiles, porcelain, and glass are expressive. They are objects to be admired, touched, and used.

The Danes' creativity is shown off through vibrant splashes of color. Some older houses are topped with golden turrets. Bright paint dazzles the eye. Almost every window has a box overflowing with brilliant scarlet geraniums. Bright red sentry boxes at Copenhagen's Rosenborg Palace complement the deep blue uniforms of the royal guard. Inside the palace are the glittering crown jewels and a collection of rare plants, each providing its own colorful imagery. One is man-made and glittering, the other rich with natural hues. One fable claims life-size lions made of silver guard the king's ivory coronation throne and watch over the country's monarchs when they die.

Left: A royal guard stands watch at Rosenborg Castle.
Right: Lovely homes and gardens along a canal in Copenhagen

So it is no wonder that the delightful tales of Hans Christian Andersen were appreciated by the Danes. They could feel the power of his words in their own hearts.

Yet good business sense has made many Danes wealthy and has contributed to one of the highest standards of living in Europe.

THE DANISH MONARCHY

There is even a fairy-tale quality about the country's rulers. Denmark has Europe's oldest monarchy, dating from at least 985. The Danes love their royal court. In the 1930s, a socialist prime minister was asked why he didn't do away with the king. He responded that King Christian X was so popular that he would be elected president anyway, if Denmark changed its political system. So the minister good-naturedly agreed that the Danes might as well keep their king.

Frederik VII, king from 1848 to 1863, gave up the absolute monarchy and presented Denmark with its first constitution in 1849. He lived by the words, "The people's love is my strength."

Danish royal blood can be found throughout Europe. In fact, during the reign of Christian IX, one of his daughters was queen of England and another was tsarina of Russia. A grandson was elected king of Norway and another was king of Greece.

The royal family has been quite "common." King Christian X loved riding his horse through downtown Copenhagen. He would often dismount and chat with his subjects. Christian never rode with any guards and always stopped for traffic lights. When he was seriously ill shortly before his death, the people in the street would stop and talk to his son, Prince Frederik, while he was shopping. They honestly wanted to know how his father was feeling.

King Frederik IX loved the sea and was an accomplished sailor.

King Frederik IX conducting the Royal Danish Orchestra (left)
and Queen Margrethe II (right)

Occasionally, he even conducted the Royal Danish Orchestra. He performed admirably, according to the newspaper critics.

Queen Margrethe II has ruled Denmark since 1972. She was one of three daughters of King Frederik IX and Queen Ingrid. The first Margrete was the strong-willed queen of Denmark, Norway, and Sweden, who built a mighty empire after the death of her husband King Haakon VI of Norway.

Today's queen is just as forceful and energetic. Her right to the throne was established with Denmark's new constitution in 1953, which allowed a woman to become Denmark's royal ruler. Margrethe has many talents. She is a noteworthy archaeologist and has participated in digs around the world. A true artist, the queen has illustrated several books, from J.R.R. Tolkien's fabled *Lord of the Rings* to Jorgen Stegelmann's delightful *Stories of Regnar Lodbrog*. In 1985, she designed a stamp that celebrated the fortieth anniversary of Denmark's liberation from the Germans.

The royal family, left to right: Prince Frederik,
Prince Henrik, Queen Margrethe, and Prince Joachim

In 1967 Margrethe married Prince Henrik, the French-born
Count Henri de Laborde Monpezat. When their oldest son
Frederik turned eighteen on May 26, 1986, he was named crown
prince and took his place in the *Statsraad*, a governmental body
consisting of the queen and her cabinet members. Frederik will
eventually succeed his mother as ruler of Denmark. Next in line
to the throne will be Prince Joachim, born in 1969.

Under the Danish system of government, the monarch must not
interfere in political matters and has no powers. However, the
king or queen appoints the prime minister, who must keep the
monarch informed of everything that is going on in the
government. The king or queen has another important duty. Only
when the monarch signs laws adopted by parliament are they
then officially in force. And according to the constitution, the
monarch must belong to the Evangelical Lutheran church, the
official church of Denmark.

The Danes are comfortable with this arrangement. Queen Margrethe and her family are considered symbols contributing to the stability of their country. As such, they are important.

THE BUSINESS OF GOVERNMENT

The executive branch of the Danish government consists of a Cabinet of Ministers headed by a prime minister. They are all responsible to the Folketing.

The Folketing is the legislative branch of government. There are 179 members, of which 135 are elected by voters in 23 electoral districts. Forty others are elected at large. Two represent the Faeroes and Greenland. The Folketing meets the first Tuesday in October, with committees handling most of the day-to-day work. Elections for the Folketing are held every four years, although the prime minister can dissolve parliament and call for an election any time if his party loses the majority. Any Danish citizen eighteen years old or older may run for office.

To stay in power, the prime minister and the Cabinet must be supported by a majority of the Folketing. If no single party has such a majority, a compromise government has to be set up. Coalitions of two or more parties then work together to form a Cabinet. The Folketing makes the laws that govern Denmark.

Unless they are members of the Folketing, Cabinet members cannot vote, although they can debate. The ministers decide public policy and affairs of state. There is even a minister of Scandinavian affairs who oversees Denmark's ties with its neighbors. The minister of the interior supervises local governments. Fourteen *amter*, counties, are the basic political units. Each has an elected council and chairman. The councils must make sure the roads are in good repair. They also supervise the schools and their county's health facilities. Copenhagen has its own town council, elected by the city residents, as well as an eleven-member executive committee appointed by the council. These are powerful positions, carrying a great deal of responsibility. Danes take their civic duties seriously. There are usually many highly qualified men and women running for office.

In 1915, the constitution was altered so women could vote and be elected. Over the following years, women took their rightful place alongside men. After the December 1990 election, four of the twenty-one Cabinet ministers were women. They headed the ministries of social affairs, cultural affairs, energy and industry, and health.

The Danish judicial system consists of ninety lower courts. The next two highest appeals courts are the *Ostre Landsret* at Copenhagen and the *Vestre Landsret* at Viborg. The Danish Supreme Court is the *Hojesteret*. Other special courts are responsible for economic and maritime cases, labor arguments, and juvenile matters. There is no death penalty for crimes in Denmark.

DANISH DEFENSE

Denmark does not have a large army. Every male citizen between the ages of nineteen and twenty-five can be drafted to serve in the military for nine months. The Danish navy is formidable, although small. It even has six submarines, as well as minelayers, torpedo boats, and destroyers.

There is also an air force, with up-to-date technology and weaponry. Many of the jet fighter planes are produced by

The royal guards in dress uniform (left) and folk high school students (right)

Sweden's SAAB works at Linköping, Sweden. The air force helicopter fleet is often requested to help in sea rescues. The military's husky Sikorsky choppers fluttering overhead are a welcome sight to anyone in danger.

The royal guards are the most colorful military unit in the Danish armed forces. They were established in 1658 to protect the royal family. Over the centuries, they have bravely performed their duty, even when it cost them their lives. On special occasions such as the queen's birthday, they replace their blue uniforms with full-dress, bright red uniforms. They wear high bearskin hats when on duty at Amalienborg Palace.

GOING TO SCHOOL

In Denmark parents don't have to send their children to school, but they must see that their children are educated for a minimum of nine years. To satisfy that requirement, a majority of parents

97

make sure their children attend primary and lower secondary classes. More than half of the children stay on for a voluntary tenth year of schooling. Pupils take lessons in geography, languages, mathematics, science, history, and literature. Sex education is required because the Danes feel that knowing about their bodies and emotions is important.

After attending the lower grades, students continue on for vocational training or become apprentices in a business. Others attend the *gymnasier*, high school.

There are many opinions concerning the best way to educate young people, and Danes are fond of expressing themselves at length on the subject. Parents have a great deal to say about how public schools operate. Each school has a board of parents and teachers who help determine what books and teaching lessons are used. Most teachers are skilled in several subjects and work with the same children throughout the year. The Danes feel that this gives a consistency to learning.

To enter college, young people face tough examinations. Candidates must study hard. A higher education is usually a requirement for a successful career in business or government.

There is a strong dedication to learning, from the fishermen on the tiniest islands to company presidents in the cities. Education is free, paid for by the high taxes.

Denmark's excellent folk high schools are known around the world. Most students are over eighteen. They live at the school and take independent study courses covering Danish government, history, and literature for up to forty weeks. No examinations or degrees are given.

Denmark has many institutions of higher learning, ranging from dental colleges to a graduate school for library science. There is a

Graduating students, wearing their white caps, dance around the equestrian statue of King Christian V.

Royal Veterinary and Agricultural University, as well as universities at Århus, Roskilde, Ålborg, and Odense. Denmark has a technical university, an engineering academy, and several institutes of music and fine arts.

It is a proud day when students receive white student caps, signifying they can be admitted to the university. When they graduate, Copenhagen students traditionally dance around the huge equestrian statue of King Christian V in Kongens Nytorv Square. The sound of folk songs fill the air as everyone celebrates.

The Royal Academy of Science and Letters and the Institute of Theoretical Physics are important research centers. Scholars from many scientific disciplines spend long hours in the laboratories there. Thousands of volumes in the Royal Library and National Archives are valuable tools for learning. Many of the books are old and rare. They provide a fascinating glimpse into the past.

The Danish astronomer Tycho Brahe made accurate observation of the planets, including plotting the orbit of Mars. Danish physicist Christian Christiansen was a putterer and a fixer. He studied refraction of light, invented a water-jet pump, and wrote excellent textbooks.

Schack August Steenberg Krogh won the Nobel Prize for medicine in 1920. He learned how capillaries expanded to permit a great flow of oxygenated blood to working muscles. This discovery was valuable for understanding how the active body works. Niels Bohr won the Nobel Prize in physics in 1922 for his work on atomic structure.

There are other important Danish doctors, geologists, zoologists, botanists, and every other type of science and medicine. All these brilliant men and women started their lifelong work in the Danish school system.

Greenland has a nine-year compulsory education system and many students continue their schooling for another four years. After compulsory school, Greenlanders can attend college in Denmark.

The people of the Faeroe Islands appreciate the mixture of being on their own and the benefits of affiliation with a larger nation. The school system on the Faeroe Islands is similar to that of the Danish mainland. Students attend primary school and move up to more specialized training in nursing, seamanship, or engineering. For other university courses, Faeroese students have to travel to Denmark.

DANISH HABITS

The Danes may appear to be a bit cool and reserved, but once you get to know them, they are warm and inviting. Family life is important.

Casual dress is the preferred attire with young people.

Danes are punctual; they like things to start on time. They believe this attitude shows good planning. It is not a question of being too disciplined. "We just like to be organized," Danes say. Professional men and women always dress carefully. There is much handshaking when anyone gets together for a meeting.

Tak, "Thank you," is probably one of the most common phrases in Denmark. Courtesy is considered necessary.

This doesn't mean that the Danes are stiff or always formal. Far from it. Young people dress casually in leather jackets, T-shirts, and blue jeans.

LOVE OF HOLIDAYS

Danes love their holidays, several of which have religious beginnings. The principal public holidays are New Year's Day, Maundy Thursday and Good Friday in Easter Week, Easter Monday, and *Store Bededag*, Prayer Day on the fourth Friday after Easter.

Left: A family dances around their Christmas tree.
Right: Dressed as a clown, a child celebrates Shrove Tuesday.

Other holidays are Liberation Day (May 5), Ascension Thursday (fortieth day after Easter), Constitution Day (June 5), Whitmonday (the seventh Monday after Easter), Christmas Day, and December 26. Christmas is the main festival of the year and the holiday children love the most. A feast of roast goose is usually served at a special Christmas Eve supper.

Youngsters get an extra day off from school on April 16 for Queen Margrethe's birthday. A favorite activity is to visit Amalienborg Square in Copenhagen to watch the royal guard on parade. The Monday before Shrove Tuesday is another favorite day, because children dress in colorful costumes and walk around their neighborhoods asking for money to buy candy. This holiday activity is similar to Halloween trick or treating in the United States.

There are other special days, as well. On May 4, the Danes mark the eve of the day celebrating the end of the occupation by the Germans in World War II. Flickering candles are prominently placed in all the windows.

The ballet and opera season at the Royal Theater begins in mid-May with a round of glamorous parties and receptions. And on Midsummer's Day, June 24, rockets are set off all over the country. This is done to scare off evil witches thought to fly over the land on Midsummer's Eve. Toward the end of June a Viking festival is held at Frederikssund, where bonfires are lighted along the coast.

Since 1912, American Independence Day on July 4 has been celebrated in Denmark. Americans of Danish descent are invited to homecoming celebrations at Rebid, near Ålborg in northern Jutland. (More than 300,000 Danes have emigrated to the United States.) A national park at Rebid is used by Danes and Danish Americans for concerts, rallies, and lectures. Thousands of guests, including the royal family, flock to a natural amphitheater in the hills, perching like gulls on the overlooks. They listen to wonderful music and meet old friends.

CHERISHED FOLKWAYS

Celebrations or festivals call for a dance. On holidays, children wear ethnic costumes if they have them. However, not many Danes have such original traditional clothing at home anymore. So folk troupes have been formed to help remember the old ways. One of the largest troupes, the Danish Country Dancing Society, was established in 1901. Today, almost fifteen thousand Danes are regular folk dancers.

Women's folk costumes consist of a bonnet, many layers of petticoats, a blouse, a jacket, and a scarf. Lace making and

Folk dancers celebrating a holiday

stitching with gold and silver thread provide delicate highlighting to the clothes. Men's costumes include knickers, white woolen socks, sweaters, and jackets.

THRILLING WORLD OF SPORTS

Every courtyard, alley, or field is a potential soccer field for Danish children. Kids play ball before school, during school, after school, on weekends, holidays, and in the summertime. Soccer is the most popular sport in Denmark, with the national team always making a strong showing when it plays other countries. Some of Denmark's top professional players have been signed by clubs in Italy, Germany, Belgium, and England. The Danish women's team won a world championship in soccer in two successive years.

One man is playing several different chess games at once.

Badminton, rugby, rifle shooting, tennis, hiking, cycling, gymnastics, sailing, rowing, swimming, and skiing demonstrate that Danes have a broad range of athletic interests. Men's and women's teams have won international archery, fencing, and rowing competitions. At least one person in four belongs to some sports club. In the 1930s women swimmers captured the imagination of their nation. Ragnhild Hveger was called the "Golden Torpedo" because she set forty-four world records. Inge Sorensen was only twelve years old when she won a bronze medal in the 200-meter breast stroke in 1936 in the Olympics.

Danish chess masters are legendary. The country's first chess club was founded in 1865, and the Danish Chess Federation was formed in 1905. Dr. O.H. Krause and Jorgen Moller were once the world's best players.

Bridge is a popular card game. Eager fans flock to national

tournaments where they can watch top players demonstrate their skill. The Danish Bridge League was organized in 1935 to coordinate these games. It is estimated that more than ten thousand players belong to 177 bridge clubs. Skillful Danish female card players have been successful internationally. They have taken medals and trophies at championship tournaments whenever they play.

Queen Margrethe is an official patron of the Athletics Awards, *Idraetsmaerket*. These are given each year to men and women who have passed tests based on age. The motto of the awards is "sport for the many and sport for many years." Trainers are educated at sports high schools—the first of which was founded in 1920 by Niels Bukh. The Danes take their sports seriously, while at the same time they have fun.

RELIGION FROM OLD TO NEW

The ancient Danes followed a Norse religion similar to that of their neighbors in Norway and Sweden. The *Eddas*, poems passed down by word-of-mouth by *skalds*, or minstrels, and finally written down by ancient chroniclers, spin tales of monsters and magic. Twelfth and thirteenth century writings, by a Dane named Saxo and Iceland's Snorri Sturluson, who set down the legends of Vikings kings, often are studied by historians for their vivid language.

At one time, the Danes worshiped the sun as a god. Priests traveled from village to village with a disk mounted on a pole that represented the power of the sun. Stone and bronze figurines have been unearthed throughout Denmark. They represent the various other gods in the Danish spiritual hierarchy. Odin was the great warrior god of the Vikings, although the god Tor or Thor was depicted more often.

The names of the old Norse gods have come down through the centuries in the names of the days of the week: *søndag*, sun or Sunday; *mandag*, moon or Monday; *tirsdag*, Ti or Tuesday; *onsdag*, Odin or Wednesday; *torsdag*, Tor or Thursday; *fredag*, Freja or Friday. Saturday is *lørdag*, washing or bathing day. Even the word *jul* or Yule, Christmas, is a gift from the Danes of long ago.

The national church in Denmark is Evangelical Lutheran. Christianity was introduced to Denmark in 826 by a Roman Catholic Benedictine monk named Ansgar who wandered north from France. His followers built their first church on the ruins of the pagan shrines. Christianity was officially adopted by the Danish royal court in 960. In that year, a monk named Poppo convinced King Harald Bluetooth that the story of Christ was more powerful than that of Odin. According to legend, the brave Poppo carried a red-hot iron in his bare hands to demonstrate his faith. Harald was so impressed he ordered all his subjects to become Roman Catholics.

Over the ensuing centuries the Roman Catholic church amassed enormous wealth and power. Many people objected to this. Subsequently, Denmark, like the rest of northern Europe, was caught up in the Protestant Reformation of the 1500s.

Unlike the rest of Europe, however, the doctrines of reformist Martin Luther were introduced from Germany with little turmoil in 1536. One of the first leaders of the new reform Danish church was Hans Taude Tausen, who was said to have been a magnificent preacher.

In keeping with their maritime heritage, many churches have ship models hanging from their ceilings or archways. Carvings of

The Marble Church, at the end of the street, is officially
named Frederikskirke, "Frederik's Church."

ships are even found on the backs of pews, where bored
youngsters whittled when they probably should have been
praying.

In 1849, freedom of religion became part of the Danish
constitution. Christians, Jews, Muslims, and other believers can
worship in peace. Christian teachings and prayer are still part of
the school day, although there is official separation of church and
state. Today, the church is maintained by a small government-
levied tax on church members. This must be paid along with
income tax. In addition, a minister for ecclesiastical affairs remains
in the prime minister's Cabinet.

About 97 percent of the population belongs to the national
church. The next largest denomination is Roman Catholic.
Seminaries for training Lutheran clergy are located at the
universities in Copenhagen and Århus. Many women are now
ordained ministers.

*Folk music (above) and old Tudor architecture (right)
are both revered and preserved.*

PAST AND FUTURE

Danes have a strong respect for the past. By keeping alive all aspects of their heritage, they ensure that their country will remain strong and proud in the future. The Danes keep a clear vision about what life is all about. Scholarship and business success are important. Yet having fun and being considerate of others are just as valuable.

This is not to say living in Denmark is as simple as a fairy tale. The Danes are the first to admit that they have as many problems

Children playing in a hay field

as any of their neighbors. For every three marriages, there are two divorces. Alcoholism and drug use have become problems. But the Danes generally tackle these hard issues with the same enthusiasm as they do other challenges. For instances, drug abusers in Copenhagen run their own rehabilitation services. Counseling services help couples whose marriages are in trouble.

Most Danes work hard to make their small country a great place in which to live now and in the future. They take care of each other, are concerned about the land, and strive for the best. They create beautiful artwork and write wonderful tales.

Opposite page: This chimney sweep is a busy man because homeowners are required to have their chimneys cleaned at least once a year.

MAP KEY

Åbenra	N11	Løgstør	M11
Ålbaek	M12	Lokken	M11
Ålborg	M11	Lolland, *island*	N12
Ålestrup	M11	Middelfart	N11
Allinge	N14	Møn, *island*	N13
Als, *island*	N11, N12	Mykines, *island*	D8
Anholt, *island*	M12	Naestved	N12
Århus	M12	Nakskov	N12
Assens	N11	Neksø	N14
Atlantic Ocean	D8, E8	Nolsoy, *island*	D8, E8
Birkerød	N13	Nørresundby	M11
Blokhus	M11	Norwegian Sea	D8
Bordoy, *island*	D8	Nyborg	N12
Bornholm, *island*	N14	Nykøbing	M11
Brønderslev	M11	Nykøbing	N12
Bulbjerg, *peak*	M11	Odense	N12
Dímunarfjørdur	E8	Randers	M12
Esbjerg	N11	Ringkøbing	M11
Eysturoy, *island*	D8	Rødbyhavn	N12
Fåborg	N12	Rømø, *island*	N11
Faeroe Islands (Føroyar)	D8, E8	Rønde	M12
Falster, *island*	N12, N13	Rønne	N14
Fanø, *island*	N11	Roskilde	N12, N13
Fredericia	N11	Rudkøbing	N12
Frederikshavn	M12	Samsø, *island*	N12
Fugloy, *island*	D8	Sandoy, *island*	E8
Fyn, *island*	N11, N12	Silkeborg	M11
Give	N11	Sjaelland, *island*	M13, N12, N13
Grenå	M12	Skaerbaek	N11
Grindsted	N11	Skagen	M12
Haderslev	N11	Skagerrak, *strait*	L11, M11
Hadsund	M12	Skanderborg	M11
Hanstholm	M11	Skive	M11
Helsingør (Elsinore)	M13	Slaettaratindur, *peak*	D8
Herning	M11	Slagelse	N12
Hillerød	N13	Sønderborg	N11
Hirtshals	M11	Streymoy, *island*	D8, E8
Hjørring	M11	Struer	M11
Holstebro	M11	Suduroy, *island*	E8
Horsens	N11	Sumba	E8
Húsavik	E8	Svendborg	N12
Hvide Sande	N11	Svinoy, *island*	D8
Jylland, *island*	M11, M12, N11, N12	Tarm	N11
Kalsoy, *island*	D8	The Sound	N13
Kalundborg	N12	Thisted	M11
Kattegat, *strait*	M12, M13	Thyborøn	M11
Klaksvík	D8	Tønder	N11
København (Copenhagen)	N13	Tórshavn	D8
Køge	N13	Tranebjerg	N12
Kolding	N11	Vágar, *island*	D8
Korsør	N12	Varde	N11
Kruså	N11	Vejle	N11
Kunoy, *island*	D8	Vestmanna	D8
Laesø, *island*	M12	Viborg	M11
Langeland, *island*	N12	Vidoy, *island*	D8
Limfjorden, *strait*	M11	Vordingborg	N12
		Westerland	N11
		Yding Skovhøj, *peak*	N11

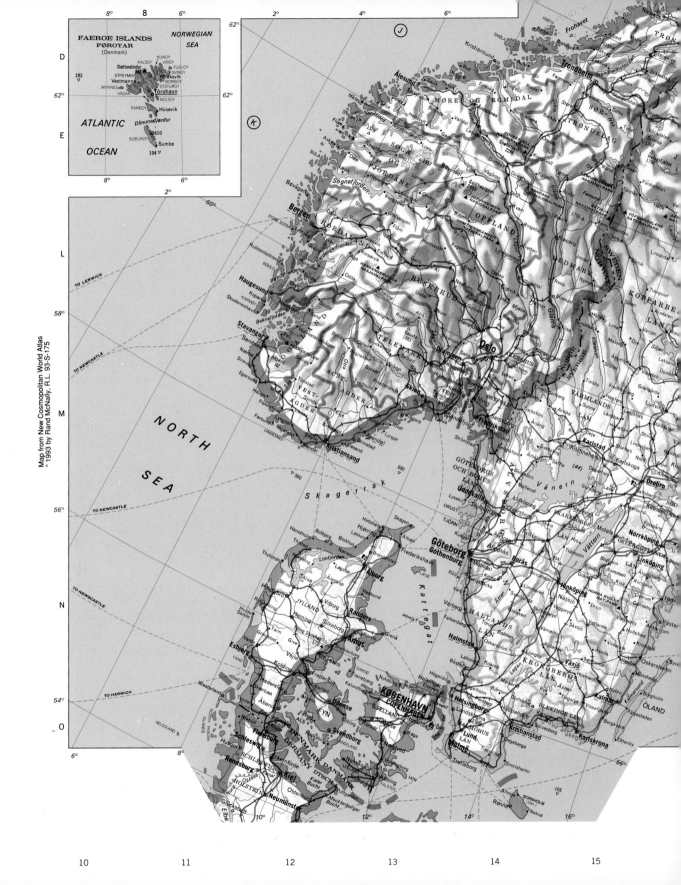

MINI-FACTS AT A GLANCE

GENERAL INFORMATION

Official Name: *Kongeriget Danmark* (Kingdom of Denmark)

Capital: Copenhagen

Government: Denmark is a parliamentary state with a constitutional monarchy. The Danish monarchy is the oldest in Europe. The king or queen is the chief of state with only ceremonial power; he or she appoints the prime minister, who is the head of government. The prime minister appoints a Cabinet of Ministers, and together they are responsible to the 179-member *Folketing*–Denmark's single-house parliament. Elections are held every four years and citizens age 18 and over can vote. The *Statsraad* is a government body consisting of the king or queen and their cabinet members. Laws adopted by the Folketing must be signed by the monarch to become official. The judicial system consists of a Supreme Court, *Hojesteret*, and ninety lower courts.

The Faeroe Islands are a province and Greenland is a self-governing part of Denmark. Both send two representatives to the Folketing; Faeroe Islanders and Greenlanders are Danish citizens. The 32-member Faroese *Lagting* (parliament) is one of the oldest legislative assemblies in Europe, dating back to Viking times.

For administrative purposes Denmark is divided into 14 *amter*, or counties, and two communes–Copenhagen and Fredericksberg.

Religion: The Evangelical Lutheran faith is the official religion, but religious freedom for all is guaranteed by the constitution. Some 97 percent of the population belong to the national church. The monarch must belong to the Lutheran church. Christian teachings and prayer are part of the school day. The Lutheran clergy is trained at the seminaries at the universities in Copenhagen and Århus; many women are ordained as Lutheran ministers.

During Viking times, Danes worshiped the sun and warrior gods. *Troldkirken* (Troll Church) near Limfjord is one of the oldest primitive shrines in Denmark.

Language: Danish is the official language but English is spoken and understood almost everywhere. Businesspeople speak fluent English and German. Several regional dialects of Danish are also in use. The Faeroese language is spoken in the Faeroe Islands, but Danish is taught as a compulsory subject in schools. The Greenlandic language is used in Greenland.

National Flag: Legend says that the Danish flag, *Dannebrog*, "the spirit of Denmark," was dropped from heaven on June 15, 1219. It is the oldest national flag to have been used continuously. The flag has a simple white cross on a red field.

The Faeroe Island flag is a red cross outlined in blue on a white background. The Greenland flag portrays the midsummer sun with red and white colors.

Money: Danish krone (dkr; plural kroner) of 100 ore is the national currency. In July 1993 one dkr was worth $0.15 in United States currency.

Weights and Measures: The metric system is in force, but some local units are used for special purposes.

Population: 5,152,000 (1993); density 310 persons per sq. mi. (120 persons per sq km); 87 percent urban, 13 percent rural. Faeroe Islands; 47,450; Greenland; 55,533

Cities:

Greater Copenhagen.. 1,337,114
Århus 200,188
Odense 138,986
Ålborg... 113,599
Torshavn (Faeroe Islands) 14,767
Nuuk (Greenland).. 12,217
(Population based on 1990 estimates.)

GEOGRAPHY

Coastline: 1,057 mi. (1,701 km)

Highest Point: Yding Skovhoj, 568 ft. (173 m)
Mt. Gunnborns, 12,247 ft. (3,733 m) (in Greenland)

Lowest Point: Sea level

Rivers: There are many short and fast-flowing rivers. The Guden is the longest (98 mi.; 158 km). Central Jutland has many small lakes; Lake Arreso is the largest, covering some 16 sq. mi. (41 sq km).

Forests: About 9 percent of the country is forested. Common trees include beech, fir, elm, maple, oak, and ash. There are no forests on Greenland, but *tundra* vegetation of moss, lichens, and grass and some stunted trees are found, especially along the southern coast.

Wildlife: There is not much wildlife as more and more area has been taken under cultivation. The wildlife consists of foxes, deer, squirrels, and rabbits. Birdlife, however, is abundant and includes ducks, partridges, and pheasants. Denmark has some 75 wildlife preserves.
Polar bears, musk oxen, wolves, lemmings, arctic foxes, reindeer, and numerous varieties of sea birds live on Greenland.

Climate: The climate is relatively mild with an average of 32° F. (0° C) in January and 62° F. (16.6° C) in July. The Danish winter is usually cool, cloudy, and humid. Rain falls fairly evenly throughout the year and averages about 24 in. (61 cm) a year.
Most of Greenland has an ice-cap climate, with all months averaging below 32° F. (0° C). Torshavn in the Faeroe Islands has the smallest range of temperature of any part of Europe; conditions remain cool and wet throughout the year.

Greatest Distance: East-West, 250 mi. (402 km)
North-South, 225 mi. (362 km)

Area: 16,633 sq. mi. (43,080 sq km)
Greenland: 844,019 sq. mi. (2,186,010 sq km)
Faeroe Islands: 540.1 sq. mi. (1,398.9 sq km)

ECONOMY AND INDUSTRY

Agriculture: About two-thirds of the country is cultivated. Danish farms are not large but utilize modern machinery. Some 8 percent of the population works on farms and produce carrots, onions, cabbages, potatoes, turnips, sugar beets, hay, oats, barley, flowers, and livestock. Cattle, pigs, sheep, and chickens are raised. Danish cattle breeds are noted for their high milk production; most crops are used as cattle feed. Danish butter and ham are considered to be the best in the world. Methods are improved constantly to make better milk and meat products.

Sheep are raised along the southern tip of Greenland and on the Faeroe Islands.

The major fish are cod, herring, norway pout, sand lances, halibut, sprat, whiting, trout, and salmon.

Fishing is important in Greenland where seal hunting is the major industry. The Faeroese also are active in fishing.

Mining: Major minerals are sand and gravel, industrial clay, chalk, and limestone. Explorations in northwest Jutland have recently established reserves of sand with titanium, zircon, and yttrium. Greenland has deposits of zinc, lead, iron ore, coal, molybdenum, cryolite, and uranium.

Manufacturing: Most Danish factories are relatively new and the equipment is regularly updated. Most of the manufacturing plants use natural gas instead of coal, and are located around Copenhagen. Chief industries are cement, beverages, automobiles, porcelain, furniture, textile, glassware, nonelectrical machinery, stereos, television sets, and silverware. Denmark is a leading manufacturer of marine diesel engines, hearing aids, controls for thermostats, and industrial enzymes.

Transportation: Denmark has a highly efficient network of roads, ports, air terminals, ferry boats, and railways. The railroad network totals about 17,820 mi. (28,678 km). The state highway system consists of some 3,000 mi. (4,828 km), in addition to 33,000 mi. (53,107 km) of secondary roads. Tunnels, bridges, and ferries provide connections across fjords and inlets separating many islands. An extensive network of public transport serves major cities; bicycles, buses, and cars provide transportation within the cities. The Langebro Bridge connects Amager island with Copenhagen. SAS, the Scandinavian Airlines System, is the joint airline of Denmark, Norway, and Sweden. The major international airport is at Kastrup, near Copenhagen. More than 35,000 ships call at the port of Copenhagen each year; other Danish ports are Århus, Ålborg, Esbjerg, Odense, and Ronne.

Communication: There are some 50 daily newspapers with a total circulation of about 1,900,000. Radio and television programming is handled by Radio Denmark, responsible to the Danish Ministry of Cultural Affairs.

Trade: Denmark has a favorable balance between imports and exports. Chief imports are heavy machinery, chemicals, and transport equipment. Major import sources are Germany, Sweden, United Kingdom, United States, and the Netherlands. Chief export items are machinery, precision instruments, agricultural products of animal origin, and chemicals. The major export destinations are Germany, Sweden, United Kingdom, France, Norway, and the United States.

EVERYDAY LIFE

Health: Denmark has a very strong health care system. Complete medical and health care is available to all Danish citizens. Scandinavian citizens can have the same health benefits and social security in all Scandinavian countries (Norway, Sweden, and Denmark). The major causes of death are heart diseases and cancers. Life expectancy at 72 years for males and 78 years for females is one of the highest in the world. The infant mortality rate at 7 per 1,000 is extremely low. In the early 1990s there were some 300 people per physician, and 164 people per hospital bed—one of the best ratios in the world.

Education: Denmark has virtually a 100 percent literacy rate. Education is not compulsory, but children are educated for a minimum of nine years. Education is free and is paid for by high taxes. Almost all children attend elementary and lower secondary classes. Compulsory subjects are geography, languages, mathematics, science, history, and literature. Students continue vocational training schools or *gymnasier* (high school) after attending the lower grades. Each school has a board of parents and teachers who help determine what books and teaching lessons are to be used. The Danish Folk High Schools give independent study courses to students over 18 years of age, but no examination or degrees are given.

There are numerous institutions of higher education. There are universities at Århus, Roskilde, Ålborg, Copenhagen, and Odense. The Royal Academy of Sciences and Letters and the Institute of Theoretical Physics are the major research centers. About 12 percent of the government budget is spent on education.

Greenland has a nine-year compulsory education system. The school system on the Faeroe Islands is similar to that of the Danish mainland.

Holidays:

January 1, New Year's Day
April 16, Queen Margrethe's birthday (only for youngsters)
May 5, Liberation Day
June 5, Constitution Day
December 25, Christmas
December 26

Movable holidays are Maundy Thursday, Good Friday, Easter Monday, Ascension Thursday, Whit Monday, and *Store Bededang,* "Prayer Day," on the fourth Friday after Easter.

Culture: Denmark has some 300 museums. The National Museum at Copenhagen is the largest. Other Copenhagen attractions are the Borsen, the oldest stock exchange building still in use in the world; the *Radhus,* "city hall"; Christiansborg fortress; the Supreme Court; the Court Theater; the Royal Library (with 125 million books); and the Amalienborg Palace complex (queen's residence). The Royal Theater runs a widely diversified schedule of drama, ballet, opera, and modern dance. The Royal Library in Copenhagen is the largest in Scandinavia.

The Danish Fire Brigade Museum, the Århus Viking Museum, and the Moesgard Prehistoric Museum are in Århus. The Louisiana Museum at Helsingor is noted for its collection of modern art; the Danish Museum of Technology is also at Helsingor. The Hans Christian Andersen Museum is at Odense. The Historico-Archaelogical Research Center of Lejre is near Roskilde and the Viking Ship Museum is at Roskilde. There are numerous theaters, with at least 72 exclusively aimed at young people. Each year a Children's Theater Festival is held near Copenhagen.

Food: Danish breakfast generally consists of cereal, cheese, or eggs. Fish and meat are the major part of lunch and dinner. A traditional Danish dish is roast duckling stuffed with apples and prunes; it is served with red cabbage and boiled potatoes. *Smorrebrod,* or open-faced sandwiches, are popular for lunches. Danish pastries are world famous; *kringle* is a nut-filled coffeecake. Danes drink coffee with most meals and in between meals; *aquavit* is a strong liquor flavored with caraway seeds.

Sports and Recreation: Soccer is the most popular sport among both men and women. Children play soccer whenever they get time. Other popular games are badminton, rugby, rifle shooting, tennis, hiking, cycling, gymnastics, archery, fencing, sailing, rowing, swimming, and skiing. At least one person in four belongs to some sports club. There are roughly 200 bridge clubs and more than ten thousand players belong to these clubs. *Idraetsmaerket* (Athletics Awards) are presented annually by Queen Margrethe. Tivoli, a world-famous amusement park in Copenhagen, is lighted with thousands of twinkling lights in the night. May 4th is celebrated with flickering candles to mark the end of the German occupation in World War II. Rockets are set off all over the country on June 24th to scare off evil witches.

Social Welfare: Denmark has one of the highest standards of living in the world. The social service network is extensive. The government spends almost half of its budget on the welfare system. Workers are paid well, but they may pay 54 percent income tax and 20 percent sales tax to cover the social services. Danish workers receive an average of five weeks paid vacation every year. Parents can each qualify for fourteen weeks of maternity leave with pay. The government operates nurseries and day care centers. Unemployment benefits can be almost 90 percent of weekly earnings. From the age of 67 each Danish citizen receives a pension from the state. For the elderly and handicapped, the government runs collective housing, sheltered housing, and full-care housing with varied levels of on-site medical and social assistance.

IMPORTANT DATES

3000 B.C.–Hunters finally settle down permanently for agriculture

A.D. 500–Vikings take many voyages to the coasts of Britain and Western Europe

800–The Faeroe Islands are populated by Irish monks

826–Christianity is introduced by a Roman Catholic Benedictine monk named Ansgar

928–The city of Århus is founded

960–Christianity is officially adopted by the Danish Royal Court; King Harald Bluetooth builds a wooden church at Roskilde

982–Eric the Red sails to Greenland from Iceland

985–The Danish monarchy begins; stone carvings tell the story of conversion to Christianity

988–The town of Odense is founded

1013-1042–Denmark rules England

1036–Faeroe Islands come under the rule of Norwegian kings

1100-1250–Almost 1,800 of Denmark's nearly 2,000 churches are built

1254–Copenhagen receives a royal charter

1282–The Danish king is forced to sign the *Handfaestning*, "The Great Charter," that establishes an annual parliament; it is the first Danish constitution

1380–A Norwegian-Danish monarchy is established under Queen Margrete I

1397–Denmark, Sweden, and Norway are united in the Union of Kalmar

1479–The University of Copenhagen is founded

1520–Sweden and Finland leave the Danish crown union

1536–Copenhagen becomes Denmark's capital; the doctrines of Martin Luther are introduced; Lutheranism becomes the official religion

1618–The beginning of the Thirty Years War, fought over religion, money, territory, and power

1648–The end of the Thirty Years War

1658–The Treaty of Roskilde between Sweden and Denmark; the royal guards are established to protect the Danish royal family

1676–Denmark defeats Sweden at the Battle of Oland

1677–Denmark wins the Koge Bay Battle

1792–Denmark becomes the first country to ban slavery in its overseas possessions

1801–Copenhagen is bombarded by the British

1805–The first forest preserve is established

1813–Denmark's economy is devastated by British naval attacks

1814–Frederik VI makes peace with Britain, Sweden, and Russia; Norway is given to Sweden; education is made compulsory

1843–Tivoli Gardens are opened

1848–A new constitution is drawn up

1849–Denmark becomes a constitutional monarchy; German-speaking Danish citizens lead a violent revolution; Prussia invades Jutland; freedom of religion to all is guaranteed by the constitution

1864–Battle of Dybbol; Denmark is defeated by Germans and loses Schleswig and Holstein provinces to Germany

1868–Esbjerg seaport is constructed on the west coast to improve trade with Britain

1871–The Danish Women Citizen's Society is formed to support women's issues; Germany is unified

1901–King Christian IX institutes numerous domestic reforms; the Danish Country Dancing Society is established

1903–The first fiction film, *The Execution*, is produced

1904–Denmark's first permanent movie house opens in Copenhagen

1911–The Association for Nature Conservation is founded

1912–The world's first oceangoing motor ship is built by Burmeister and Wain, Denmark's largest industrial firm

1915–A constitutional amendment gives Danish women the right to vote

1920–Denmark's current borders are established; Schack August Steenberg Krogh wins the Nobel Prize for medicine; the first sports high school is formed; North Schleswig is returned to Denmark

1933–Denmark's political parties agree on emergency measures to help people during the Great Depression; the International Court of Justice declares Greenland an official part of Denmark; the University of Århus is founded

1939–A Government Film Office is set up to purchase and distribute educational and documentary films; Denmark is forced to sign a nonaggression pact with Germany; Adolf Hitler invades Poland

1940–Hitler attacks Denmark

1944–Iceland gains independence; Johannes Vilhelm Jensen is awarded the Nobel Prize for literature; the Germans blow up most of Tivoli Gardens

1945–Germany surrenders; World War II is over (started 1939)

1946–The Faeroe Islands Parliament votes for independence

1948–The Faeroe Islands are granted Home Rule

1949–Denmark joins the North Atlantic Treaty Organization (NATO)

1953–The Danish constitution is revised, the Upper Chamber is abolished; a single chamber of Parliament is established; a woman is allowed to be the ruler of Denmark; a new constitution makes Greenland a province

1955–The first government ombudsman is appointed

1958–Louisiana Museum is founded at Helsingor; industrial exports exceed agricultural exports for the first time; the Education Act is passed

1959–Denmark joins the European Free Trade Association (EFTA); the Socialist People's party is formed

1961–The Ministry of Cultural Affairs is established

1962–Helsinki Agreement on Nordic Cooperation is signed with Denmark as a founding member

1964–National Endowment for the Arts is set up

1965–Danish Film Foundation is established

1966–Odense University is founded

1967–Queen Margrethe II marries Prince Henrik

1970–The Christian People's party is founded

1971–Scandinavian countries sign an agreement to share their cultural identity

1972–King Frederik IX dies, Queen Margrethe II succeeds to the Danish throne; Roskilde University is founded; Denmark resigns from EFTA

1973–Denmark joins the European Community (EC); equal pay for both men and women for the same job becomes a legal requirement; abortion is legalized

1974–The National Endowment for the Arts is updated; the Environmental Protection Act is passed

1976–The Social Assistance Act is passed

1978–A referendum reduces the voting age from 21 to 18

1979–Greenland receives Home Rule similar to the Faeroe Islands

1990–General elections are held; an expedition finds several World War II Allied fighter and bomber planes under deep snow in Greenland

1992–Danish voters reject the European Community's so-called Maastricht Treaty (Treaty on European Union) toward closer integration of European countries

1993–Prime Minister Poul Schluter resigns; Danish voters ratify the Maastricht Treaty in a second referendum; Tivoli Gardens celebrates its 150th birthday

IMPORTANT PEOPLE

Jeppe Aakjaer (1866-1930), poet and novelist

Hans Christian Andersen (1805-75), master of fairy tales; work includes *The Little Mermaid*, *The Emperor's New Clothes*, *The Ugly Duckling*, *The Red Shoes*, and *The Tinder Box*

Ansgar (801?-865), monk who introduced Christianity in Denmark in 826

Bille August, film director; his film *Pelle the Conqueror* won the Oscar for best foreign-language film

Fredrik Bajer (1837-1922), winner of the Nobel Peace Prize in 1908; founded Danish Peace Society (1882) and International Peace Bureau (1891)

Baroness Karen Dinesen Blixen (1885-1962), writer; wrote under pen name of Isak Dinesen and Pierre Andrezel; works include her personal memoirs *Out of Africa* and *Seven Gothic Tales*

Harold August Bohr (1887-1951), mathematician; brother of Niels Bohr; formulated Bohr-Landau theorem

Niels Henrik David Bohr (1885-1962), physicist; winner of Nobel Prize for physics in 1922

Niels Aage Bohr (1922-   ), physicist; son of Niels Bohr; shared 1975 Nobel Prize for physics with Benjamin Mottelson

Napoleon Bonaparte (1769-1821), French emperor

Victor Borge (1909-   ), concert pianist/entertainer

August Bournonville (1805-79), dancer and choreographer; originated the Danish ballet style; director of Royal Danish Ballet

Tycho Brahe (1546-1601), astronomer

George Morris Brandes (1842-1927), leading European literary critic

Erik Bruhn (1928-86), dancer and choreographer; known for his classic technique; directed ballets at the Royal Swedish Opera House and the National Ballet of Canada

Diderik Buxtehude (1637-1707), musician and organist

Henning Carlsen (1927-   ), Danish filmmaker

Grethe Krogh Christensen, musician; professor at the Royal Danish Conservatory

Christian II (1481-1559), king of Denmark and Norway (1513-23); considered the first modern king of Denmark; also called Christian the Tyrant; exiled and died in imprisonment

Christian III (1503-1559), king of Denmark and Norway (1534-59); adopted the Lutheran faith as the state religion; Denmark became fully Protestant under his rule

Christian IV (1577-1648), king of Denmark and Norway (1588-1648); led Denmark during the Thirty Years War

Christian V (1646-1699), king of Denmark and Norway (1670-99); attempted to regain lost territories from Sweden

Christian IX (1818-1906), king of Denmark (1863-1906); led to Denmark's defeat at the Battle of Dybbol

Christian X (1870-1947), king of Denmark (1912-47) and Iceland (1918-44)

Christian Christiansen (1843-1917), Danish physicist; studied refraction of light and invented a water-jet pump

Carl Peter Henrik Dam (1895-1976), biochemist; winner of the Nobel Prize in medicine in 1944

Carl Dreyer (1889-1968), film director; films include *The Passion of Joan of Arc* (1928), *Day of Wrath*, and *Ordet*

Eric the Red (late 10th century), a Norseman from Iceland who gave Greenland its name to lure settlers

Erik of Pomerania (c.1381-1459), grandson of Margaret I; elected king of Denmark

Edvard Eriksen, a sculptor; most famous sculpture is the bronze Little Mermaid overlooking Copenhagen harbor

Johannes Ewald (1743-1781), one of Denmark's greatest lyric poets of the 18th century; work includes *Adam og Eva* (1769); wrote Danish national anthem "Kong Cristian" in 1779

Johannes A.G. Fibiger (1867-1928), physician; winner of the Nobel Prize in medicine in 1926

Niels Ryberg Finsen (1860-1904), physician; winner of the Nobel Prize for medicine in 1903

Fleming Ole Flindt (1936-   ), dancer; director of Danish Ballet

Frederik III (1609-1670), reigned from 1648 to 1670; became the first absolute monarch of Denmark (1660); ended the tradition of elected kings; declared his descendants will always rule Denmark; laid the foundation of the Danish museum system, instituted the unified legal system, established schools, and developed transportation routes

Frederik VII (1808-1863), king of Denmark from 1848 to 1863; during his reign the absolute monarchy ended and power was shared between the monarch and the Rigsdag

Frederik IX (1899-1972), son of Christian X and father of Queen Margrethe II; also an accomplished sailor and musician

Crown Prince Frederik (1968-   ), first born of Queen Margrethe II; named crown prince in 1986

Povla Frijsh (-1960), soprano

Niels Gade (1817-90), musician and composer

Karl Adolph Gjellerup (1857-1919), writer; shared the Nobel Prize for literature with Henrik Pontoppidan in 1917

Nikolai Frederik Severin Grundtvig (1783-1872), romantic poet and religious thinker; founder of Danish Folk High Schools

Thomasine Gyllembourg, feminist author

Haakon VI (1340-1380), Norwegian king; husband of Margaret I and father of Olaf II

King Harald Bluetooth (c.910-c.985), one of the Danish Viking kings; supported the introduction of Christianity in Denmark

William Heinesen (1900-   ), Faeroe Island writer

Prince Henrik, full name Count Henri de Laborde Monpezat; Queen Margrethe II's husband

Adolf Hitler (1889-1945), politician; dictator of Nazi Germany

Ludvig Holberg (1684-1754), classic writer, historian, philosopher, and critic; also known as father of modern Danish literature

Arne Jacobsen (1902-71), architect; designed SAS building in Copenhagen

Jens Peter Jacobsen (1847-85), novelist and poet

Johannes Vilhelm Jensen (1873-1950), poet and novelist; winner of Nobel Prize for literature in 1944 for his series of novels

Prince Joachim (1969-   ), second son of Queen Margrethe II

Niels Juel (1620-1697), Danish admiral who defeated Sweden at the Battle of Oland

Soren Aabye Kierkegaard (1813-55), philosopher and theologian; works include *Repetition, Either/Or* (both written in 1843), and *Stages on Life's Way* (1845)

Schack August Steenberg Krogh (1874-1949), physiologist; winner of Nobel Prize for medicine in 1920

Martin Luther (1483-1546), German religious reformer; founder of Protestantism

Queen Margrete I (1353-1412), daughter of King Valdemar IV; queen regent for her son Olaf II; after Olaf's death, became queen of both Norway and Denmark; wife of King Haakon VI of Norway

Queen Margrethe II (1940-   ), daughter of Frederick IX, ruling queen of Denmark since 1972; also a noteworthy archaeologist and artist

Lauritz Melchior (1890-1973), musician; leading tenor at the Metropolitan Opera at New York from 1925 to 1950

Benjamin Mottelson (1926-), physicist; shared the Nobel Prize for physics in 1975 with Aage Niels Bohr

Martin Anderson Nexö (1869-1954), author; works include *Pelle the Conqueror* (1906-10) and *Ditte* (1917-21)

Carl Nielsen (1865-1931), composer and conductor; work includes the comic opera *Maskarade*

Odin, a Viking deity

Adam G. Oehlenschlaeger (1779-1850), poet and dramatist

Hans Christian Orsted (1777-1851), physicist; discoverer of electromagnetism

Henril Pontoppidan (1857-1943), writer; shared the Nobel Prize for literature with Karl Adolph Gjellerup in 1917

Poppo, a Christian monk who convinced King Harald Bluetooth that the story of Christ was more powerful than that of the Viking god Odin

Knud Johan Victor Rasmussen (1879-1933), explorer and anthropologist; an authority on Eskimo ethnology

Poul Nyrup Rasmussen, a Social Democrat; prime minister since 1993; a former economist for the Confederation of Danish Trade Unions

Ole Romer (1644-1710), astronomer

Aksel Schiotz (1906-75), musician

Poul Halmskov Schluter (1929-), conservative prime minister from 1982 to 1993

Hans Taude Tausen (1494-1561), called the Danish Luther; one of the early preachers of the reform Danish church

Thor, a Viking deity always depicted carrying a mighty hammer; he is Odin's son

Bertel Thorvaldsen (1770-1844), Danish sculptor; specialized in the Greek style of lifelike creations; most famous sculpture is the statue of Christ in the Church of Our Lady in Copenhagen

Jorn Utzon (1918-   ), Danish designer and architect; works include the famous saillike vaults of the Sydney Opera House, Australia

Valdemar I (1131-82), called the Victorious; a Danish king; he instituted a law code and established Denmark's first census

Valdemar IV (c.1320-1375), Danish king under whom Denmark became a mighty sea power

Compiled by Chandrika Kaul

About the Author

Martin Hintz, a former newspaper reporter, has written more than a dozen books for young people. The subjects range from training elephants to other titles included in the Enchantment of the World series. He and his family live in Milwaukee, Wisconsin. Hintz has a master's degree in journalism and is a professional travel writer/ photographer who has won numerous awards for his work.

For their help in background information, the author would like to thank the editors of *The Danish Journal;* the Danish Film Institute; the Press and Cultural Relations departments of the Royal Danish Ministry of Foreign Affairs; the Danish Ministry of Education; the Danish Ministry for Greenland; and the staff of the Embassy of Denmark, especially cultural attaché Bent Skou. The author appreciates the assistance of Professor Niels Ingwersen, chairman of the Scandinavian Studies Department of the University of Wisconsin-Madison and Professor Bo Elbrond-Bek of the Scandinavian Department at the University of Washington, Seattle. The author also wishes to thank Arne Melchior, former Danish minister of Transport, Communication and Public Works; travel journalists Ian Gimble and Nina Nelson; author Bent Rying; and the publishers of *Baedeker's Denmark.*